RAHKAL C. D. SHELTON

WOOSAH

REVISED EDITION

A SURVIVAL GUIDE FOR
WOMEN OF COLOR WORKING IN CORPORATE

Printed in the United States of America

ISBN: 978-0-578-56538-5

Rahkal C. D. Shelton
Lawrenceville, Georgia 30043

Woosah
www.rahkalshelton.com/woosah

Instagram: rcarladanielle
Twitter: rcarladanielle
Facebook.com/rahkal.shelton
www.youtube.com/c/rahkalshelton

Cover Illustration: Nancy Devard
Editing: Bettye Underwood
Typesetting: Kathy Curtis

Some identifying details, passages, and scenarios have been
changed to protect the privacy of individuals.

TABLE OF CONTENTS

Acknowledgments.. vii

Author's Note... ix

Introduction xiii

Chapter One   I Fired My Employer 1

Chapter Two   The Playing Field................................... 25

Chapter Three Self-Worth Is Net-Worth...................... 41

Chapter Four   Identifying Toxicity and
Taking Action!... 55

Chapter Five   Managing Stress! 85

Chapter Six   Boundaries!... 99

Chapter Seven Communities and Tribes 125

Chapter Eight Woosah 139

Bonus   Affirmations for Thriving in the
Workplace 151

About the Author 157

References 159

DEDICATION

To our culture and every black and brown-skinned girl who has ever questioned her *magic*—You are more than enough, and you can conquer anything.

ACKNOWLEDGMENTS

Many wonderful people and some not so wonderful experiences have contributed to my desire and need to write this book. First and foremost, I would like to give honor to my Lord and Savior Jesus Christ. I acknowledge that apart from Him, I am and can do nothing! Lord, thank you for always sustaining, protecting, and loving me.

Every facet of this process has delivered the most appropriate people right when I needed them: Nurse Tina Williams, Dr. Caren Ogle, and Dr. Malaika Berkeley, along with my friends, former colleagues, "cackling hens," besties, and close family members. I would also like to thank my loving sister Rachel for being a coach, champion, and refuge for me.

Special thanks to Dr. Joe L. Roberson Jr. I couldn't have done any of this without you. I appreciate your support, sacrifices, coaching sessions, love, and patience.

To my former colleagues, supervisors, and professional associates: Thank you for every good and bad experience. Each encounter not only led me to this point, but also gave me an opportunity to grow. And to all my supporters, mentees, and readers: Thank you for your unwavering support.

Special thanks to the creatives who worked on this project, including my cover illustrator, editors, and layout designer. If I am forgetting anyone, please charge it to my mind and not my heart. Much love.

AUTHOR'S NOTE

So you've finally picked up your copy of *Woosah: A Survival Guide for Women of Color Working In Corporate.* First off, thank you! You're in for a treat, as this is *Woosah's* third revision. Much has changed personally since I first wrote this book in 2019. My knowledge, perspective, maturity, and comfort level in discussing this topic have evolved immensely. In 2023, it appears that some women of color who have experienced racism in the workplace are more hopeful. Since the pandemic and the public execution of George Floyd, our country has come to a much-needed racial reckoning. We've had significant open dialogues on race, DEI programs implemented, Juneteenth recognized as a federal holiday, and minority grant opportunities galore. All good, considering slow progress is better than none. Right?

However, on the flip side, many women of color are still in the throes of frustration stemming from discrimination, microaggressions, being underpaid, racist remarks, and covert competency quizzes. And these women are hurt, angry, and looking for solutions to better show up authentically while obtaining workplace peace. These are the women I'm here for.

My purpose for adding this author's note to *Woosah* is to share my current perspective on racism and expound on my intentions for *Woosah*. Woosah is a verb that speaks to taking a breather. It's gathering yourself and hitting the reset button. And admittingly, we all can use a Woosah from time to time.

The book addresses the painful experiences and impacts of discrimination, unconscious and implicit biases, and systematic racial issues rooted in hate. I'm talking about our country's bitter battle with racism and how it hovers in many workplaces.

Racism is one of those things that we just can't stay silent about, pretend it never happens, or that it's over. Hate is the root of racism, and hate infiltrates our workplaces, classrooms, courtrooms, and boardrooms. It's a sickening disease that only causes pain, division, and missed opportunities to see each other's humanity. There is a way to engage the topic while firmly holding people and systems accountable and without contention.

I believe racism can be cured with love, healthy conversations, kindness, open hearts, accountability, antiracism, and empathetic gestures but over time. Addressing racism doesn't have to be divisive; to nonminority readers, just because something isn't your experience doesn't mean it isn't someone else's experience. I believe much of the problem with racist behaviors lies with superiority complexes, a lack of humility, and discrediting another's experience because they don't share that same experience.

Talking about issues impacting women of color in the workplace with positive intent, humility, a willingness to stand against racism, and solution-based approaches helps to eradicate complicities even when unintentional. It's time to get off the fence of "avoiding politics or ruffling feathers," racism isn't political. Our country made it that way.

Racism is a threat to all humanity. I wrote *Woosah: A Survival Guide for Women of Color Working In Corporate* to encourage healthy dialogue to educate, inspire, provide a voice for, and validate an underserved group of women. I wanted *Woosah* to serve as a primer for younger women of color, specifically first-gen college-educated black women entering the workforce.

So far, *Woosah* has garnered features in Forbes and HuffPost, while continuing to inspire women to be more confident in their diverse authenticity while speaking up and protecting their peace. I also released an accompanying workbook titled *Woosah Workplace Peace: 7 Keys to Obtaining a More Fulfilling Work Experience*, as additional support that provides more resources tailored to help women of color brainstorm, plan, and execute clear strategies for workplace fulfillment. After firing my corporate employer, I vowed to educate and empower black and brown women, helping them navigate injustices while rising above them authentically.

Hey, work environments can be stressful all by themselves, so the added pressures that women of color face only worsen matters. I want to see all women thriving and confidently identifying and owning their God-given purpose in and out of the workplace. I especially want to see black and brown women do the same without unnecessary obstacles.

I hope this book inspires more organization, intentionality, and preparation to thrive professionally. And I know If you commit to doing the work, get the workbook, and advocate for yourself, you'll see transformational results.

Be Blessed,
Rahk

INTRODUCTION

B eing a woman is tough enough by itself. With all of life's demands vying for our immediate attention, we are, at times, hardly able to juggle all of our responsibilities—our job tasks, our families, our homes, our children, spouses, and ourselves. Then, there's the workplace, and with everything combined it can feel like walking on a tightrope with neither a harness to hold us up nor a protective mat to catch us if we fall.

Some women experience an additional stringent layer to these demands than others; the common denominator for the women with these stringencies look just like me, if not many shades lighter or darker. I'm referring to women of color. Working in corporate environments, specifically for women of color, can be gut-wrenching. It is impossible to ignore the many factors that contribute to this phenomenon. We often have to navigate through underestimation, undervaluing, gender gaps, disrespect, microaggression, discrimination, biases, and toxic environments resulting in these factors. And to make matters worse, in many cases we are underpaid.

So, you ask, how can black and brown women navigate the corporate world while maintaining our sanity, peace, health, and the *magic* we bring (which, of course, is the very essence of who we are as people, working women, and women of color)? Look no further; help is in your hand.

Woosah, at its core, is about preserving and safeguarding your mindset and emotions. It's about *you,* knowing your worth, voice, and contributions while protecting your sense of peace. Consider me your *goalfriend* or a *sistafriend* you're having a candid conversation with about work life. I promise to keep it honest. In this book, we will explore strategies, stories, and tips on how to thrive in the workplace. Use this book as a guide for navigating through toxic environments, boundary setting, work culture, and anything that threatens your health, happiness, and success.

By the end of our journey, you'll have some practical tools designed to take you from surviving to thriving in the workplace. First, let's woosah…In other words, take a deep breath, hold it, and then exhale. As you release the air from your lungs, reflect on who you are and how your sacrifices have helped you reach this point in time. You got this, girl! You are stronger than you know. You are a woman of color. You can be, do, survive, and conquer everything while still maintaining your sense of peace.

And I promise that if you follow (and I mean really follow) this godsend of a guide, you'll have a stronger sense of awareness, assuredness and a keen ability to better manage work relationships, work stress, and anything else that work life throws your way.

In preparation for writing this book, I spoke with twelve women of color. Most importantly, I took an in-depth look at the 12+ years I dedicated to the workplace. Well, Sis, I had a real come-to-Jesus moment, during which I reflected on all of my encounters, experiences, lessons, and failures.

After thinking the familiar refrain, *I wish I knew then what I know now,* I began to ponder, *How can I use this information to support other women of color working in corporate America?*

I didn't want to base the entire book on just my personal experiences. And, chile, I have stories for days! But, my most insightful conversations were the ones I had with the twelve women I mentioned above. Most of these women were former colleagues, professional associates, and friends. Others were senior or intermediate managers, or fresh out of college and just beginning their careers. Even though the women resided in different cities and worked for different corporations, a common theme rested in each one of their stories.

All the feedback was very similar, forcing me to come to a single conclusion. Now, understand this wasn't a conclusion that I hadn't already figured out through my own experiences of working in corporate America as a black woman. However, my conversations with the twelve women did provide me with the validation I needed to ensure that I wasn't tripping, disillusioned, or "grasping at straws."

I knew I wasn't the only minority sista who could attest to the drama and stressful experiences caused by management, colleagues, work demands, and the *unwritten* policies commonly found in most corporations. However, I can only speak from my own experiences and the observations and conversations I have had with other career-oriented women of color.

My Granny used to say, "Tell the truth and shame the devil. Share what you have been through and help someone else." Well, Granny, I am telling *my* truth and shaming devilish behavior so I can empower others to tell theirs.

The truth is that my experiences have taught me the value and significance of speaking up, and creating and sustaining a healthy work culture headspace. Additionally, I now clearly understand the need for effective leadership to "weed out" toxicity and minimize the stress caused by gossipy and lazy colleagues, a lack of clear boundaries, heavy workloads, unhealthy work environments, unrealistic expectations, etc. Please understand that it's usually the workplace environment that prompts great workers to walk out the door and into hospitals, finally ending up on therapy couches, overeating or drinking.

Yep, it's also crazy clients, incompetent bosses and strict deadlines stretching us thin, as well as biases and racial factors. But work environments and work culture is *everything*. You can't stay silent, Sis. I know my experiences have taught me the value of disrupting the status quo—we *must* speak up. I only wish I had done it sooner. I'd be lying if I said I have all the answers, because I don't. However, I'm eager to share my story and some of the things I wish I had known *before* I started working in corporate America.

This book was created from my desire to boldly "pay it forward," inspire, and encourage other individuals who are struggling to thrive in corporate America and various workplaces. I got tired of wearing a mask every day and passively moving about. People often say, "Hindsight is 20/20," and I couldn't agree more.

Now that I'm in a position of reflection, the mask is off, and the politically correct muzzle has been removed from my mouth. As a result, I now feel lighter, healthier, and more peaceful. I can finally see and speak confidently. I've also realized just how applicable *Woosah* is for every workplace. Period. So when you read corporate America, just replace it with workplace. Deal?

CHAPTER ONE

I FIRED MY EMPLOYER

It's been exactly three weeks since I unceremoniously fired my employer. Yep, I turned in my resignation with all of the peace, positive energy, good juju, and confidence I could muster. On my last day, I returned my badge, cellphone, laptop, and corporate American Express card before pulling out of the parking lot. What was I listening to on my way out? Chris Brown's "Deuces."

Hiding behind my oversized dark aviator shades, I took in every melody, note, and emotion behind those lyrics. Why? Because they resonated deeply in my soul. In other words, I totally felt like a *superSHEro*, dressed in high-waisted leather pants and a sexy pair of patent leather stilettos. I was *that* chick—the one who causally and calmly walks away from the massive explosion popping in the background. Yeah, her. Well, that chick was me...at least in my head...until I got home that afternoon.

1

I remember thinking, "I wonder what will happen next and what will happen to my savings…" It dawned on me just how fast my hard-earned savings would deplete, but surprisingly, it didn't make me feel anxious. I literally had zero regrets, because I knew I had made the right decision. Instead of being fearful, I was nervously excited about my next endeavor. Seriously.

So, I'd officially been home for one week…cleaning, doing laundry, reflecting, strategizing, and occasionally twiddling my thumbs. Well, technically, I was not twiddling my thumbs, more like processing everything, and I arrived at a conclusion. What was my big revelation, you ask? I decided it was time to write another book—not any old book, but a book that would help others with their professional lives and the workplace. This was a particularly good idea because writing has always been a form of therapy and a source of peace for me.

"Wow, girl! You *finally* did it! I am so proud of you!" said the voice on the other end of the phone line. "What a boss move to take care of you. Hopefully, you won't be eating Ramen noodles next month. Ha-ha, I'm kidding with you, girl! I know things will work out for you. They always do."

Don't you just love friends? Seriously, I really do have great friends. You know, the kind who look out for the people they love and care about. My friends not only know how to be supportive; they also know precisely what to say to motivate and inspire me. Sometimes I get the impression they think of me as superwoman, that I can do anything. At least that's how they make me feel... even when I don't feel very amazing or courageous.

In fact, I was trying to get a handle on prioritizing and organizing each day—what it should look like and involve. As you probably guessed, I have lots to do. And as embarrassing as it is, I recognize how *institutionalized* I have become after working in corporate for so long. The truth is, it's hard not to be critical of myself. As a creative person, it's been challenging to flow, be organic, and breathe, even if I am unable to reach my self-imposed deadlines. Sadly, however, I have become accustomed to working under stressful conditions, being underestimated, having others mistrust my judgment, being micromanaged, and wearing a mask while performing job duties. So, to be out of the office and fully liberated from these downers takes a little adjusting. Honestly, this freedom allows me to do the things I am most passionate about—inspiring and serving others. It's been a long time coming.

For this, I am thankful. Not everyone has the gall or guts to leave a job with nothing lined up, but I've done it before. This time, I chose to focus on my mental and physical health rather than stay in an environment where I'm stressed, overworked, underpaid and underappreci-ated. Honestly, I really wasn't in a position to leave my job, but I knew I needed to make a move. I felt as if my life depended on it. If I stayed any longer, I would've lost more of myself, i.e., my drive and confidence. And there's a good chance I would have eventually snapped, making the 6PM news...in handcuffs. I say that with all sarcasm. Seriously, you have to be able to read the writing on the wall. If a *space* can alter your physical, mental, and emotional health and wellbeing, it has way too much power over you. Because I am also a woman of great faith, I understand that God has no intention of abandoning me, now or ever. You won't be abandoned, either.

I left corporate America, firing my employer for two reasons:

1. I read time well, so I knew it was time to go. I had worn out my welcome and had hit an emotional and developmental ceiling in my position. I would have considered staying longer, but *only* in a different capacity and *only* for the pay, health insurance, and other benefits. And although I wasn't initially aware of it, I was trading time with my passion and loved ones for a steady paycheck. Many people feel stuck in a role for this same reason.

2. The toxicity of the environment *and* the stress that comes with "playing the game" (i.e., office politics, wearing a mask, and suppressing my authentic voice), microaggressions, being an *only* (my brown and black sistas know what I'm talking about), the corporate culture, and the lack of advancement, advocating and representation for black people, was just too exhausting for me. This isn't just a reference to my last employer, but practically every employer and experience I have had since my professional career began. This

drama heavily affected my mental and physical wellbeing.

"Culture is more important than simply a vision. Some leaders have great vision, but have created a toxic culture where that vision will never happen."   –Phil Cooke

Let me start by saying this: I understand that everyone's experience is and will be different, and we won't all see things the same. That is a fact! But I wish I had had a guide or manual…or one of those "In case of emergency, break glass" kit before or shortly after I started my working career, specifically in the broadcast industry. But, no…I had nothing to warn me about what I was really entering into. I had no clue what to expect or what working in this environment—as a black woman—would truly entail.

I was "green" and fresh out of college, so I truly believed that "word is bond." In other words, I assumed people meant what they said, and were decent, moral, fair, and at a minimum, respectful human beings. I also thought my internships, experience, and possession of a graduate degree meant something, and that it would ultimately help me advance up the corporate ladder. But sadly, I was wrong—so wrong.

I probably reeked of Enfamil formula and Gerber baby food to the powers that be and my non-minority colleagues. Or, possibly the privileged afforded to them via the color of their skin, superiority complexes, and white supremacy prevented them from seeing me at all. I really didn't have an inkling about how savage, "dog-eat-dog," disrespectful, dishonest, bias and cutthroat some employers, companies, and corporate work environments could be, especially toward women of color. I am pretty sure my Latina, Asian, and Indian sistas can attest to similar drama and ruthlessness experienced within the corporate world. However, I can only speak of my own experiences and observations as a black woman working within a corporate setting.

Overall, it's a Catch-22 for women of color—an over-and-above tricky dichotomy. Why? Well, there is an unwritten set of rules we *must* abide by if we want to progress, advance, be comfortable or simply be respected and taken seriously. We have to know how to artfully present ourselves as both non-threatening *and* highly approachable. We're likely editing ourselves and slaves to methodically considering the optics of our hairstyles, attire, energy, body language and even the octaves in our voice when speaking.

We often feel overwhelming pressure to "play the game"—and to play it well. According to American political scientist Harold Lasswell, office politics (also known as "the game") involve undocumented rules that govern who gets what, when, and how (Lasswell, 2018). The game determines who will get a bonus, promotion, extra work-from-home days, a bigger budget, and a role in the boss's decisions—and who will not. So, not only are women of color forced to censor themselves but we must also "play the game" better than others while being at a disadvantage in terms of winning.

So much of our livelihoods depend on these "undocumented rules" that were not created for us in the first place. Think about it. We are playing a game that wasn't even designed for us—a game that involves "unwritten rules" that often conflict with our moral and emotional compass and even "official" company policies. That being said, doesn't it seem like this "game" is "fixed" and unfair for women of color?

Let's look at an example of this unjust "game" in motion. Your boss casually mentions to you and your colleagues that she is having a housewarming party this weekend. You are the only WOC in this conversation and during this conversation, she also mentions that she wishes she had a couple of hands to help her with it.

A few of your colleagues immediately offer to serve drinks during the party and clean up afterward. You are *uninterested, uncomfortable,* and *unavailable,* so you remain silent. The truth is, you don't feel good about crossing professional and personal boundaries, and you also don't believe in providing free labor.

Shortly after the party, you notice that the colleagues who volunteered to help are now acting "buddy-buddy" with your boss. She then assigns them to special projects, a desired "perk"…but you, on the other hand, aren't offered any plum assignments.

What happened here?

Most companies don't necessarily prohibit personal relationships but do have policies against any behavior that could be perceived as a conflict of interest, as well as anti-harassment. The purpose of these policies is to prevent employees from feeling obligated to their supervisors in any way, or pressured into doing something they're uncomfortable with. However, it still happens, because that's just the way "the game" goes sometimes. This is a minor but typical example of you choosing set boundaries but paying for it negatively.

In addition to "playing the game," black women are also expected to be docile while simultaneously appearing open and inviting in the workplace.

For example, we are expected to smile, speak in pleasant, non-confrontational tones, and passively share our feedback—after others have already spoken, of course, to avoid being labeled "aggressive." Basically, every cell in our bodies must scream, "I'm safe!" to make our employers and colleagues feel more comfortable around us. And, guess what? Many of us are willing to go above and beyond to do just that. We also tend to say, "yes" when asked to do tasks, even though we know we may have to figure it out on the fly with little to no support or direction. For black women, everything is figureoutable. Oh, and learning to filter through indirect, passive-aggressive directives while remaining enthusiastic, that's a priceless jewel. I have been tasked with this type of responsibility so many times I've lost count.

For example, I was once asked to report to my boss's office. Now, keep in mind, I was literally the first black woman in this particular position, and I was the *only* black woman sitting on that team and in that area.

Disclaimer: Occasionally, I'll share an individual's race to paint a more vivid picture of my point of view and to highlight my encounters with implicit biases as a black woman working in corporate America.

Did you notice this book cover? Of course, you did. That cover is a direct reflection of what *I* have experienced in the corporate landscape. As a matter of fact, I believe it's safe to say it's a direct reflection of how many people of color working in corporate America have to cope. Yes, turning our backs to unnecessary drama and surveillance while identifying a space of peace...taking a Woosah. Woosah for me speaks to resetting, clearing your mind, and decompressing before taking another stab at the task at hand.

Am I racist for my illustration? Absolutely not, and unfortunately, I have been on the receiving end of numerous encounters at work where race was the common denominator. I believe it is important to use these experiences as "teachable moments."

Let's return to the example...

Ah, yes summoned to the boss's office. There was a director (a white woman) I previously worked with (not *for*) who had an uncanny knack for treating me like I was her intern or personal assistant. This woman was notorious for suggesting a task, setting very specific requirements for the task (in her head), and then *vaguely* asking me for support to complete it. Wait...*what?* For instance, she once said to me, "Hey Rahkal, do you think you can research the process of relocating an employee to Atlanta, and then let me know what you find? Thanks!" I smiled, of course, and replied with, "Sure thing!" Then, I pushed aside what I was already working on to start this research for her. And, because I've been conditioned to go above and beyond what was asked of me, I even included relocation links, copied from the company's website, to the email.

Ironically, I didn't realize there was a problem—until I was abruptly called to my boss's office (another white woman and friends with the director). Well, come to find out the director did not feel that I fully understood my role and questioned my ability to perform my job duties. *Whaaaaat?!* What I didn't know at the time was that this particular director had voiced concerns about my judgment for quite some time. What the... The nerve!

To my knowledge, each time the director asked me to perform a task or asked me a question, I thoroughly responded to all requests in a timely manner. This particular instance was no different. I did exactly what she asked me to do—researched information on relocating to Atlanta. In fact, I not only did the research but also provided her with important references.

Well, after my boss brought these "concerns" to my attention, suggested coaching and asked me to "follow through in the future," it dawned on me that what she *really* wanted me to do was research relocation steps *and* start the paperwork, book the hotel and flight, create shipping labels to have the new hire's belongings shipped, and offer other relocation assistance.

This "disconnect" was astronomical. She had often given very indirect requests, and sadly, I'm not the greatest mind reader. Scenarios like this that happened frequently—i.e., passive suggestions, indirect requests, and being "voluntold" (you know...when you're told to do something, but the request or demand appears to be voluntary...wink, wink). Well, as the *only* woman of color in many situations like this, I wondered if my colleagues were just too afraid to be direct with me. Maybe, I didn't provide enough fluff or came across unapproachable where she needed to report me when I thought I was doing a stellar job. All of this often crossed my mind, but I told myself maybe I am just tripping.

Eventually, and through trial and error, I managed to partially crack the code but this required additional exhausting effort. I figured out how to better navigate requests and more effectively execute the tasks associated with them. So, the message of this story is that black women don't do well with vague expectations. *Lesson learned the hard way.*

The fact is, black women (and men, for that matter) usually have to work twice as hard as whites (males and females), to avoid inaccurate and unfair stereotypes. You know what I mean... that *all* blacks, but especially black women, are lazy, incompetent, sassy, mean, and "full of attitude."

And God forbid we change our hairstyle, because if we do, we *must* be prepared for an "unofficial" press conference about it. We *must not* get offended when one of our non-minority colleagues points out how our hair has changed, and we *must not* get upset when they impulsively try to touch it. And we most certainly *must not*

11

become offended when one of our white colleagues tells us how *lucky* we are to have dark skin and not have to tan to get "dark." Seriously?

We are also *not* allowed to get upset over "racial jokes" or discussions that focus on cultural differences, racial injustices, issues affecting minorities, and unfair stereotypical perceptions of us—which, by the way, are often discussed in front of us as if we aren't in the room or within listening distance. Seriously? Oh, and blatant differences of opinion are completely "off-limits." We aren't allowed to have thoughts, feelings, and opinions on politics and other topics, and if we do, we'd better keep them to ourselves—if we know what's good for us.

And, guess what? We have to be familiar with mainstream white actors and actresses, music, and movies just to stay relevant with our white colleagues and to be a good culture fit. Seriously? *Yes,* seriously!

For example, one day my white colleagues were discussing a performing artist who was coming to town and how desperate they were to snag some extra tickets to his concert. I stayed quiet, because I didn't know who the artist was, much less have any interest in getting tickets to his show. One of my white colleagues, a news anchor, decided to make a joke about me being silent because I didn't know who the artist was. She looked at me and said, "Poor thing is looking like...*who's* coming to town?" Her snide remark caused everyone to laugh hilariously *at* me—not *with* me. Yes, I was embarrassed, but I learned a very valuable lesson that day: Knowing more about white people stuff, the latest zombie movies and when a super-hot country music artist is coming to town can give you "skin in the game." In other words, it can keep you afloat when dragged into conversations you couldn't care less about. #Shutupalready

Apparently, it's entertaining when a person of color is too quiet and not contributing anything "meaningful" to conversations that highlight their interest. I wonder how the white news anchor who called me out would have responded had our roles been reversed. What if I had approached her and asked if she had an extra ticket to the Mary J. Blige or Jhené Aiko concert? Or, what if I asked my work team if they had seen "gangsta" movies like *Paid in Full* or *Hustle & Flow*. What if I had given them funny looks after they told me they didn't even know who those artists were or what those movies were about? What if I mumbled, "Poor thing..."? Yeah, that probably would have *never* happened.

Well, the worst thing that can happen to black and brown women is to be labeled "disruptive" or to be called into HR for being "racially insensitive" or causing "discomfort" to colleagues of other ethnicities. And, if we try to engage in equity conversations with our non-minority colleagues, candidly sharing our thoughts and feelings on various issues, we can expect it to be a "problem." (It's generally best to leave your politics at home, but for anyone working for the news media like me, it's a tough subject to avoid.)

Here's a funny, but true story: One day, a colleague of mine passionately recounted the story of a man who had slit the throat of a golden retriever because he felt *threatened* by it. Now, this colleague went waaaay out of her way to tell me about what happened to this dog. She was really upset that the man wasn't convicted and "got off" for killing an animal.

She turned to me with flushed cheeks and said, "What's wrong with people? A man killed an innocent dog because he felt *threatened.* And, guess what? That poor mama dog had just had puppies! Now, those sweet babies are going to have to grow up without their mama. And that psychopath didn't even get convicted! Rahkal, he killed an innocent dog because he felt *threatened!* Some justice system we have here."

Now, it occurred to me that a person has to get up close and personal to a dog in order to slit its throat, something hard to do if the dog is "threatening," i.e., growling ominously as it checks you out. That alone made me doubt the man's story; I suspected he just felt like killing a dog... the same way some people just look for excuses to kill people of color. But instead of pointing that out, I shook my head at the hypocrisy and replied, "Yeah...I know how it feels when people use the 'I felt threatened' line to get off for murdering people of color in cold blood. But that poor dog and her motherless puppies."

There was no way for me to accurately express how I felt about her diatribe. I wanted to make this a "teachable moment" and educate her on the harsh realities that people of color face every day due to other people's "discomfort," But I knew she wouldn't have understood, because that is not the world she lives in. If I had approached her desk the way she did mine, and passionately shared my thoughts, feelings, beliefs, and opinions about how innocent black and brown males are gunned down every day and how it hurts my heart that their killers are "getting off" for their crimes, she would have probably become highly "uncomfortable," had a panic attack, *and* reported me to HR.

So, how did I defuse the situation? By not saying much. Now, don't get me wrong; I was thoroughly pissed. I was miffed by her privilege—the same privilege that gave her the confidence to share her passionate perspectives, uninvited, with me. Meanwhile, I was *forced* to remain silent—having to carefully *pick* and *choose* my words and battles. These instances are all too common for us people of color. As a result of these experiences, I learned that there is little room available for us to share our beliefs—at least without receiving the backlash of "white guilt" or accusations of "reverse racism." In other words, if we are too direct or passionate, we risk being unfairly labeled as aggressive, angry, and/or problematic.

In my experience of working at a news station, trust me, I've heard it all. An opinion for every headline that aired. You can only imagine the types of remarks I heard from my privileged colleagues—statements I absolutely did not agree with and which made me very uncomfort-able. Let me say this—there is nothing wrong with sharing thoughts and opinions; however, I have learned that sharing them is most problematic when *we* share *ours*.

One of my tasks at the news station was to monitor what went to air. I'll be honest—it was one of the most depressing roles I've ever had. And if you haven't been under a rock the past five years, you have most likely witnessed a disturbing racial climate, unrelenting racial tension, senseless murders of unarmed black men and women (Sandra Bland and Breonna Taylor), deliberately misleading police reports, continuous protests, and insane acquittals.

In 2015, Walter Scott, an unarmed black man in South Carolina, was murdered, shot in the back several times by a white officer, following a traffic stop for a non-functioning brake light. Because my primary task was to monitor what went to air, I was required to watch the video of the shooting over and over again. Honestly, I probably watched him die at least 100 times. Every time I watched Scott's lifeless body fall to the ground (for millions to see) it not only hurt my heart; I also found it extremely traumatizing. The harsh reality of racial profiling, inequalities and the hate shown to black people in this country angers me. In the months before Scott's murder, several other unarmed black males were killed by cops, including Eric Garner, Tony Robinson, Michael Brown, and the youngest of this unfortunate group, Tamir Rice, a 12-year-old playing at a park. There are also the many instances of black-on-black crime; these anger me too. The news constantly airs tragic stories detailing the loss of life in black communities.

Less than a year later, Harambe, a gorilla at the Cincinnati Zoo, grabbed a three-year-old boy and dragged him around the enclosure. The little boy had climbed into the enclosed space created for Harambe. A staffer was forced to shoot Harambe to protect the child. Many news outlets (including ours) refused to air the gorilla's shooting, citing the "sensitive nature" of the killing.

I remember people mourning the death of this animal more intensely than the loss of human life. But what I found most troubling was how Walter Scott's death repeatedly played on the air, but the killing of a gorilla was deemed "too sensitive" to be shown even once. Think about it—an animal was treated with more respect than a black man.

I also remember discreetly crying, quickly wiping away tears before my colleagues noticed them. I called in sick to work the following day after watching the video of Walter Scott die over and over. It was almost too heavy a burden for me to bear.

Walter Scott could have been my dad, uncle, or big brother. His senseless and racially motivated murder affected me gravely—even though I didn't know him personally. I am still tied to him and can identify with both him and his story. The same goes for George Floyd and Ahmaud Arbery's murder. They all were unarmed Black males.

While working in the broadcast industry, I witnessed and heard many disheartening headlines and bias narratives daily. Just because I encountered these things firsthand in the newsroom doesn't mean these experiences are restricted to one industry. Many black and brown people in different industries share similar stories. Many of my friends, associates, colleagues, and relatives tell me that they, too, are enraged at how people of color are treated and portrayed in this country. We cry for our families, our future, our children, and we cry because of the public humiliation we have been forced to endure, as a people. In fact, almost every day, a white person calls the cops on a person of color—for no real reason. This is what happened to Christian Cooper, a black man enjoying a day of bird watching in Central Park. Christian asked a white Amy Cooper (no relation) to put her dog on a leash. Amy refused to put her dog on a leash so Christian started recording her on his phone. Amy, upset that she was asked to abide by the law (by a black man), called the cops on him and pretended to be in danger and attacked by him. Yea, pretty pathetic. Get this. Amy was a VP at the company that she worked for, but we will dive deeper into this deceitful, racist and privileged heifer later.

There's no safe space to go when we're feeling stressed and overwhelmed by the reality of potentially being the next victim person of color in America. Mental health checks and grief counseling are not offered to us on the job when our communities are struck by trage-dies. Examples of this are the 9/11 terrorist attacks, the Sandy Hook shootings, and the more recent Pulse night-club and Las Vegas music festival shooting. After those tragedies, my employer (at the time) sent out an internal communication, encouraging employees to be mindful of their mental health, self-care, and possible PTSD-inflicted psychological distress from seeing disturbing images in the media. We were reminded that grief counselors were available at our beck and call if we needed them. However, this type of support did not exist for those affected by the shooting at Emanuel AME Church in Charleston, South

Carolina, where nine black people were viciously gunned down at Bible study by a young white male. It also wasn't offered when similar tragedies—tragedies that involved black and brown people—occurred. Although I no longer work in corporate, these resources still were not offered by my former employer after recent black murders that sent our country in a tizzy. I know because I've checked with my black friends still employed.

> "Injustice anywhere is a threat to justice everywhere. We are caught in an inescapable network of mutuality, tied in a single garment of destiny. Whatever affects one directly, affects all indirectly."   – Rev. Dr. Martin Luther King, Jr.

I care deeply about the issues affecting the world, and specifically, the black community. However, I don't feel we get enough support or acknowledgment at the workplace. During the 2020 reemergence of Black Lives Matter, many employers have sent out public statements on social media. While the statements are appreciated, they simply are not enough. It's gravely important for companies to speak directly to their black employees to show they care or at minimal to stand in solidarity with them. How do you issue generic statements to the public but do not address who's in house? Black people are burden with heaviness, frustration, sadness, hurt, fear for safety of ourselves and loved ones. Many of us lack faith, trust, and hope in our justice system and country to do the right thing.

The only difference today are the rolling cameras and social media platforms' disseminating video. Now, imagine living like this with an expectation to perform well in the workplace, thrive, trust, be successful, and to be enthusiastic while working with colleagues who don't understand your plight, demonstrate empathy or even care.

Not only is this challenging, but it's also an unrealistic expectation. This is why employers need to be very intentional in times like this and all the time.

Left to cope with the influx of senseless tragedies, many of us cover our facial expressions with our mask. We suppress our voice. The truth is, I have been outraged many times over various events while sitting in the newsroom, but stayed quiet because I felt like I needed my job. More specifically, I didn't want to put a target on my back, despite having a lot to say about how we aired specific stories. I have watched people who decided to speak out against injustice, discrimination, and partiality at work undergo intense scrutiny. I've watched people get blacklisted for sharing their thoughts, beliefs, opinions, and feelings. I simply didn't feel safe enough to speak my mind.

How do you feel when you experience situations that make you uncomfortable, yet you remain silent?

Not only can women of color *not* be passionate at work, regardless of the subject or situation, but there is hardly any room to express our genuine authenticity, because if we try, we risk appearing unprofessional to others. That happened to me a couple of times. In fact, once again, I was called to my boss's office (the same white woman I discussed previously), but this time another manager, one of her direct reports (a black man), was also there. This happened during my second month on the job. I was told that a client (a middle-aged white woman) had referred to me as "aggressive." Maybe she felt intimidated because I asked for clear directives in order to effectively perform my job functions. Maybe she was buying into black woman stereotypes…Who knows?

But, after experiencing the relocation debacle, I was careful about how I handled my non-minority colleagues. The only thing I had said to my accuser was, "I work best with clear expectations for optimal effectiveness. If there is something you need, please share it directly with me." Of course, I added the fluff of smiling and using positive non-verbal body gestures, etc. *Aggressive?!* I am hyper-conscious of my image in the workplace, so I'm pretty sure I wasn't aggressive toward the woman. Assertive? Absolutely, but the woman must have had an unconscious bias towards me that caused her to see me as aggressive. My request was professional, polite, and fair. Period.

You can imagine how blindsided and discouraged I was after being summoned to my boss's office and reprimanded a second time—both within the first two months of my employment. In all honesty, I am one of the most diplomatic, positive, and professional people I know. My boss never even asked me for my thoughts on the situation. Instead, she made the black manager (her direct report) lecture me on the importance of optics, as if I were the driver of a vehicle and the manager was a driving instructor, while my boss sat and watched from the back seat. But at the time, I didn't realize the magnitude of what it meant for my boss to ask another manager—who just happened to be a black male—to reprimand me while she observed. Now, I can think of several reasons for her action. Maybe she felt intimidated by me and thought it best to get someone who looked like me to speak with me about the issue, or perhaps she simply didn't want to deal with me.

Either way, it was a terrible decision that I perceived as cowardly and offensive. That client and I had spoken twice at best. I worked very hard to be friendly to her and disarm her so I could make a great first impression. Yet, she *still* reported me for being "aggressive."

Frustrated? Black and brown women must hold their frustrations in, too. We have to keep our masks on at all times. We have to remain pleasant, even when we disagree. We are required to be unemotional, keep a can-do attitude, figure it out, and maintain a positive spirit, even under seemingly impossible circumstances. And, by all means, we *must* avoid being dubbed an "angry black woman." Oh, and one more thing…we *must* be consciously aware of how we dress at the workplace.

Black women in corporate America *must* make sure their attire is appropriate, and definitely not too snug. And, if you're curvy, like me, your skirts *must* be longer than knee-length, in case it rides up. Lastly, we *must* avoid appearing over-sexualized. We *definitely* don't want that. We experience enough over-sexualization, which only serves to reinforce unfair and inaccurate stereotypes of women in general, and black women in particular.

If you're not a minority, you may be wondering why I so frequently mention race. Yes, it's come up quite often… but, guess what? There'll be more. You see, this book is personal and predominantly inspired by the experiences of minorities while working in corporate America. It is a survival guide for women of color, predominately black women. So, I suggest you get comfy when it comes to me addressing race, because it's not going anywhere. My hope is that my experiences will help others see through a broader lens. I believe it's essential to be aware and honest about what we are dealing with, even if you personally don't participate in this behavior. And if you don't participate in this behavior but you're silent about those (you know) who do, you are participating in this behavior. Being non-racist is not enough nowadays. In order to move this country forward everyone must be **antiracist.** I also believe that it's important to be vigilant of the systems and behaviors that we are up against.

Do I believe my former employers are racist? I'm not sure. However, the companies I worked for failed miserably at recruiting people of color and promoting diversity and inclusion. As a matter of fact, my former company's president had no black direct reports. There were also no black executive producers or black senior vice presidents. In my last role there were only two black people in management and zero in upper management. This might have changed since my departure…but I highly doubt it.

This little golden nugget of information is terrifying for people of color, especially blacks. This is why being antiracist is equally important because it's easy to become complicit in silence. I have witnessed black colleagues of mine being treated differently than my non-black colleagues, even on minuscule levels. Some of these observations triggered my desire to write this book, and interviewing professional women from a wide range of fields only solidified my sentiments.

This book is not limited to just black and brown women, or even the corporate sector. It can also be applied to government, non-profit agencies, and practically every other work environment. Maybe you're a man of color…or perhaps you are a white person who could also benefit from these workplace survival tips and some self-examinations. You're welcome.

It is my goal to extend my voice and a helping hand as you or someone you care about navigates the workplace. Then again, maybe you are one of the lucky ones who have not been "burned" by your job, or corporate America. Maybe you are new to the field and looking for a job. Maybe you love what you do. Or, maybe you are hoping to glean a new perspective and insightful information from this book. Whatever the case may be, I am offering direct tips on how to thrive in your career despite your race and gender. I hope you learn, grow, reflect and become empowered.

CHAPTER TWO

THE PLAYING FIELD

B efore diving into the essence of this book and survival strategies, let's talk about the playing field. You'll need both a better understanding and a point of reference, as we identify the landscapes many of us work in. There are a couple of inherited constants that make the playing field for black and brown women more difficult to navigate than for others. Some of these constants include discrimination, unconscious bias, gender gaps, systematic racism, educational inadequacies, and income/wealth gaps.

Let's dive in!

I. Racial & Color Discrimination
The US Equal Employment Opportunity Commission defines racial and color discrimination as treating people such as applicants or employees unfavorably because he or she is of a certain race *or* because of personal characteristics associated with a specific race—i.e., hair texture,

skin color, and/or certain facial features. Color discrimination involves treating a person unfavorably because of his or her skin color. Race and color discrimination also involve treating a person unfavorably because he or she is married to (or associated with) a person of a particular race or color (US Equal Employment Opportunity Commission, 2019).

While there are laws in place to prevent these discriminatory acts from occurring, they still happen daily. Because workplace discrimination is illegal, it is often carried out covertly or masked behind some sort of irrational justification. It may sound like the following example: "Well, Tanya, the competition was stiff, but we ultimately decided to go in a different direction..." So, who did they end up promoting instead of you? A former trainee, Nicole. Now, Nicole isn't as sharp, punctual, or professional as you, *and* she has a history of tardiness and poor performance reviews. She is a hot mess! You, on the other hand, are intelligent, punctual, very professional, and have excellent performance reviews. The only other difference between the two of you is her ethnicity. The company definitely decided to go another direction... in the direction of someone they felt more comfortable with—someone who can further their agenda. Yeah, the competition was stiff—so stiff that they chose a non-minority with a less than stellar performance record over a minority with an exceptional one. Got it.

"We chose a candidate who had a slight edge over you..." What edge? Because Nicole is always the last one to show up for work and the first one to leave at the end of the day. She never completes her tasks and calls in sick fairly frequently. Is that the edge they are referring to? In contrast, you are always on time to work, stay late to make sure all of your tasks are completed and haven't taken a day off that wasn't scheduled in advance in two years.

If you are a person of color, you have probably experienced or witnessed the scenarios above. The sad part is that racial and color discrimination is hard to decipher when masked by pleasantries, if it isn't blunt or overt, which leads me to my next point...

2. Unconscious/Implicit Biases

These biases also happen frequently. The difference between racial discrimination and unconscious bias is the subtlety and the fact that these biases are unintentional. Unconscious bias is automatic. They are subconscious prejudices that have been learned, stereotypes, and invalid judgments against a person or group. Unintentional biases are also deeply rooted and influential toward behaviors.

Studies suggest that most first impressions are not only formed quickly, but are also hard to let go of. Factors like voice, attire, physical appearance, and emotional state trigger one's perception of something or someone. You may not believe this, but others formed an opinion or impression of you the moment you entered the building. Unfortunately, there is not much you can do to control first impressions. People often develop unconscious biases based on first impressions.

It is unfortunate that unconscious biases tend to be exhibited toward those in minority groups, and center on race, class, gender, age, disabilities, and religious beliefs. People are more likely to fall back on what they know, believe, or have heard, especially when making decisions, than venture into unknown territories and think or do something different. Therefore, decision makers, especially nonminority ones, *must* intentionally strategize, self-assess, reflect, and implement excellent judgment during the hiring process.

Speaking of which, some companies have begun to offer courses on unconscious bias and conscious inclusion. My former employer started to require that employees take courses on unconscious bias, diversity, and conscious inclusion. Ironically, however, most of the instructors were non-minority, so that kind of defeated the purpose. Go figure.

I believe topics that have to do with diversity and workplace discrimination are most beneficial when they are taught by individuals who are most affected by this behavior—minority instructors. *Duh.* It would be nice to have a Black, Latino, or Asian teach one or two of these courses. Why? Because, there is a good chance he or she has actually been on the receiving end of racism, workplace discrimination, and unconscious biases, allowing them to teach from experience. It's like having white instructors teach black history at an HBCU (historically black college or university).

Hopefully, the instructors teaching the diversity courses at your job are *real*, *practical*, *relatable*, and *authentic.* If this isn't the case, challenge what you're being taught. Give a couple of pointers, draft fresh scenarios and offer them. **Disclaimer**: I'm not trying to throw shade at the instructors from my former company; however, I *am* shading the infrastructure behind these courses. So, my other advice would be to make a strong and impactful first impression—i.e., highlight your strengths and be assertive, honest, and open. But although these strategies may be helpful to you, honestly, there is no right way to combat or prevent unconscious biases.

3. The Gender Gap & Systematic Racism

The gender pay gap is the difference between men's and women's salaries. Now, think about how this gap may impact brown and black women. Many, if not most, women of color experience racism and sexism simultaneously. As a result, we are often forced to attain advanced degrees and more extensive experience to boost our chances of snagging higher-paying jobs or advancing in our current positions. Why? Well first, it is important to examine and discuss the ramifications of systematic racism. Systematic racism in the simplest form is the impact from all the racist ideas, policies, laws, practices and rules that our country was founded on now trickled down into present-day standards within society, organizations and institutions. Because of America's horrific racist history and ugly past, black people are still paying the price today.

Therefore, systematic racism leads to issues like discrimination in criminal justice, policing, employment, housing, health care, politics and education, among other issues. And historically, black and brown children have always had a higher dropout rate in high school and college than white children. Granted, many minorities have and will defy statistics and historical measures and earn their high school diplomas and college degrees, but it will likely be more challenging for them later in life when it comes to getting their first job. And if they do not enter the workforce with a solid education, it will most likely be harder to land a good job, period.

Some of the fault lies on public school education; many schools tend to be under-budgeted, overly crowded, and/or lack resources, so they are working with bare bones. Teachers can't invest a lot of time in students who need extra motivation, support and attention because there isn't enough time. Students in many of the public school system are also faced with challenging adult-sized social issues such as hunger, poverty, and domestic issues. Now, don't get me wrong—there's nothing wrong with a public school education, especially if that is all you have access to and the gaps are supplemented (I myself am a successful product of the public school system). But if your experience was anything like mine, your school was under-funded, understaffed, and under-resourced, thus making it difficult to foster a more efficient learning environment. If a child doesn't have exposure, access, resources, funding, quality educators, learning necessities or support, they're less likely to graduate or be set up for success. Then there are inequalities in disciplinary, suspension and expulsion rates for black and brown vs. white kids.

According to the US department of education, black kids are suspended and expelled three times more than white kids. Black kids are also referred at higher rates to law enforcement and arresting than white kids ages K-12 (school-to-prison pipeline). Students facing these issues are more likely to drop out of school.

Please understand that school and educational inequalities are rooted in institutional and systemic racism.

At this point, you're probably thinking, "What does education and public schools have to do with anything?" Well, the answer is a lot. Systematic racism is the reason why people of color are often working two and three times harder. We are playing catchup.

Furthermore, the topic right now is the playing field. Guess what? Playing the field, having access to resources, and being in a competitive learning environment prepares people for the workforce. Unfortunately, many children of color, children residing in poverty-stricken neighborhoods, single-parent homes, and/or homes where the head of household is uneducated are less likely to attend college, be prepared for the workforce, and see racism and educational variables as a driving force of gender gaps.

2018 Women in the Workplace Statistics

- Only 1 in 25 C-Suite leaders is a woman of color (C-suite as in CEO, CFO, COO, CIO).
- Four in 10 black women never interact with superiors about their work.
- For every 100 men promoted to manager, only 60 black women are promoted to this position.
- Black women experience microaggression in the workplace more frequently than white women.
- Approximately 40% of black women have had their judgment questioned in their area of expertise.
- Only 35% of black women believe their managers showcase their achievements and accomplishments to others.

4. The Income Gap

The income gap refers to the "gap" in earnings between two groups, such as working whites and blacks. There is also the "wealth gap." However, this gap differs from the income gap, because the wealth gap refers to assets minus debts, instead of just income alone. Let's explore the income gap with black and brown women specifically. Let's also determine where we stand regarding wealth, income, and work. Understanding these gaps helps provide you with more insight as to why black and brown women are *forced* to work twice as hard to attain success.

Many of us are merely playing catch-up; we are hoping to "catch up" or at least stabilize. I want as many women of color to experience a fresh slice of the American pie as possible—not just get stuck with refrigerated leftovers. According to the Economic Policy Institute, approximately 25% of black homes have zero or negative net worth, while only 10% of white families are *that* poor (Jones, 2017). Since so many black families either own nothing or are in debt, the average wealth for the entire race declines. As a result, black families have $5.04 in net worth for every $100 held by white families (Jones, 2017).

There she goes again, some of you may be thinking. But the question is, why do we keep constantly comparing ourselves to white people, and what does race have to do with money? Well, it's not that we *want* to compare ourselves to white people—it's just that it is imperative for us to understand these facts if we are to co-exist or rise within our communities and the world we live in.

The truth is that everyone isn't going to be an entrepreneur, run a family business, or work for themselves—nor will everyone want to. Some individuals love their jobs—i.e., where they are in life and what they are doing, while others are unsatisfied with their current status. Some prefer working for others, while others prefer to work for themselves. Regardless of what you ultimately choose to do, it is important that you, at minimum, be treated with respect, compensated for your time and effort, and be granted equal opportunity to advance.

Prime Gap & Systematic Examples

At 24 years old, Becky inherited a paid-off house worth $300,000 which she promptly moved into. A 529 college savings plan had been established for her at birth that was continuously growing. Her parents paid for her college, so she had no student loan debt. Her parents were in a position to do these things because their parents set them up for success. Then Becky landed a job with a salary of $55,000 per year.

On the other hand, Keisha, also 24 years old, earns $70,000 per year, but rents a condo and owes a whopping $100,000 in student loans after earning a Master's degree. In an effort to be more competitive in her field and earn more money, she returned to school for her Master's, which is what pushed her college debt up to six figures. Keisha's hard-working parents weren't able to leave her a home or pay off her college debt. Keisha's great-grandparents were slaves and her grandparents were raised during Jim Crow. Consequently, they were subject to a plethora of blatant inequalities making it difficult to set her parents up for greater success.

If we are speaking solely in terms of income, Keisha makes more money than Becky. However, when we look at Becky's and Keisha's "wealth," it's evident that Keisha has more debt than Becky. The bottom line? Becky has a higher net worth than Keisha.

Critics who are wealthy may not understand or care to understand the importance of wealth gaps—or how they are created and maintained. You can turn on talk radio or the news and hear conservative pundits questioning why blacks just don't "pick themselves up by their bootstraps." The thing is that these pundits have no idea or regard for the stark realities people of color have inherited or face on a daily basis. Many black and brown individuals bust their butts every single day, even if we earn less than our white colleagues. Helloooo! Therefore, wealth and income gaps *must* be taken into consideration when suggesting we need to "just pick ourselves up."

The wealth gap that black people experience stems from our country's historical injustices. Historical injustices like slavery, segregation, gentrification, a lack of access, and discriminatory practices when it comes to business loans, home loans, and other funding resources contribute to the lack of wealth in minority communities. If Keisha's grandparents weren't discriminated against and able to purchase a home and receive equal pay they would have been better positioned to leave assets for her parents. While whites are able to accumulate wealth and pass it on to subsequent generations (hence the valuable property Becky inherited), the children of black and brown families usually have to start from scratch. This type of imbalance keeps Keisha financially lagging, even though she draws a larger salary than Becky. And, guess what? Neither woman is at fault. They are simply playing the cards they have been dealt.

Consider the uneducated black and brown women who make under $40k per year and who have children, along with the single parents, because they, too, struggle to attain wealth. The next generation inherits this disparity and passes it on to the generation after that, and so on. In our community, we call this a generational curse. It is this "curse" that often perpetuates income gaps, thus limiting resources that could be allocated toward education, funding start-up businesses, buying homes, supplying college funds, and providing opportunities for professional advancement.

I have heard many of my white colleagues say, "It's 2019. Isn't racism over yet?" Not only do I beg to differ, but I felt compelled, from the combination of my own experiences, misconceptions publicized by the news and circulated on social media, along with disrespectful, racially charged rhetoric from the Commander-in-Chief (as of 2019) toward minorities, to write this book. I also wrote this book for those who have experienced racism, discrimination, unconscious biases, and outright prejudices, because the effects of it will impact future generations.

Keisha, determined to do things the "right way" and follow the path to the "American Dream," learned a harsh reality—that education doesn't always balance the playing field that is the workforce. She also learned that the "American Dream" isn't as readily available for everyone, even if that person works twice as hard as everyone else.

By the way, Keisha was passed over for a promotion due to a combination of unconscious bias and discrimination. Even though she was well-qualified for the position, had a great rapport with her team, and was an extremely strong contender for the job, she was unable to snag the promotion. Instead, inexperienced, "fresh out of college" Karen won the hard-sought promotion. Now, it's important to point out that Karen was the daughter of the hiring manager's dentist. Karen was paid a salary that exceeded Keisha's by $5k. Moral of the story—education does not guarantee that black and brown women will receive fair pay and does not protect them against the wealth gap and unconscious biases that exist in the workplace.

According to a recent study by Demos (2017), an organization that supports and provides funding for a fair, inclusive, multiracial democracy, reported the median white high school dropout has wealth similar to that of the median black adult who graduated high school and attended at least some college. It is important to also consider barriers many black and brown women face when choosing to attain an advanced education. Many of these women are *forced* to make tough decisions—leaving their families for college vs. attending less competitive local schools…paying out-of-pocket vs. acquiring hefty student loan debt. Another option is choosing to juggle a full-time job with part-time college classes, which can delay attaining their degree by years and limit their earning power for the duration, because until they get that degree they're not qualified for better career opportunities.

I faced these issues myself, and it was rough leaving my family to attend a respected college. As an oldest child, I played a fundamental role in the household. Because I was a first-generation student, I had to figure this out on my own. I also didn't have a college savings plan like Becky. Therefore, having to choose school over helping at home was extremely suffocating and discouraging. What makes this even more disheartening is that acquiring a college degree is not a guarantee of future success. In fact, many black and brown girls are forced to learn this the hard way—after working twice as hard in corporate America while being one of the most, if not *the* most educated, underpaid, undervalued, and underrepresented employees at the company (with lots of student debt to pay back).

Okay, so now that I've thoroughly depressed you with some of the obstacles you're up against, let's talk about the good stuff. The good news is that there is always *hope* and your job doesn't determine your value. Remember, you are a woman of color, which means you are resilient, creative, persevering, and *magical*. We are used to coming out on top and making something out of nothing—even in the worst of circumstances.

#Askyourancestors

Activity time! Let's take a quick inventory of your work environment.

1. **How many people of color are in leadership positions at your place of employment?**

   _____

   _____

2. **What are some of their titles?**

   _____

   _____

3. **What is the average salary range for your title/position? Where are you on the spectrum?**

   _____

4. **Speak transparently with trusted friends and colleagues about their earnings. Compare what you earn (this is to help you assess compensation).**

5. **Verify with HR whether you are on the higher or lower-paid end of your pay range. LinkedIn, PayScale, Indeed, and Salary.com are great references.**

6. Think of three accomplishments, skills, or supporting points to point out when asking for a raise.

7. Research strategies on how to ask for more money.

8. Research certifications, courses, and ways to increase your worth.

9. Finally, just do it (ask for more money)!

What's the worst that can happen? You can be told "No."

For a deeper dive, more robust activities, and lesson plans, be sure to get your copy of The Woosah Workbook and Journal, which includes 7 keys to obtaining a more fulfilling work experience. Available at rahkalshelton. com.

CHAPTER THREE

SELF-WORTH IS
NET-WORTH

You Are on The Menu

We have all heard the phrase "bring something to the table" or "having a seat at the table," but have you ever considered coming empty-handed or bypassing a seat altogether? Maybe, just maybe, *you* are on the menu, the entrée or you *are* the table. In other words, what if others needed to bring something to or glean something from *you? This is how you must see yourself.*

I don't understand why people are fighting to sit at this proverbial table in the first place. We don't even know who's doing the cooking, who prepared the table, or if that person even washed his or her hands. What if we don't want to eat at this "table?" What if we were our own tables and *we* were on the menu? What am I talking about, you ask? I'm talking about having confidence in what you bring, your skills and capabilities. By default, your essence is diversified, not just because you're a woman of color, but also because there is only one of you. You are emphatically like no other, which is the epitome of *diversity*.

Diversity is what strengthens companies, while marginalization is what stifles expansion. Diverse companies are better equipped to appeal to talented job candidates because they respect, reflect and celebrate different ideas, perspectives, and backgrounds. Diverse approaches create stronger and more productive work environments, thus delivering better results.

Let that marinate for a minute. I hope you are "smelling" what I'm cooking, "eating" what I'm baking, and are not confused by my kitchen analogies ☺. I just wish I had entered the corporate arena with this thought process; If I had, I wouldn't have fought for a seat at the table. As a result, I would have been less stressed, and my career might have played out differently. My hope is that I can guide you to a better path. I had no resources, silenced myself, and "ate" what I was fed, because I didn't think there was another option. Many times, I didn't realize others were feeding me.

You may be feeling some of the pressures that I mentioned earlier as well. For example, you may not feel that you're being your authentic self when at the job. You may feel that you're wearing a mask and a muzzle, that you keep going above and beyond to ensure that others feel comfortable. Maybe you feel that you go out of your way to be perceived as very friendly, and that you're always super inviting. If it's forced, you are acting out of character in your attempts to appease your colleagues. Is your goal to avoid being perceived as aggressive, sassy, or the "angry black woman"?

If you feel like you have to put on a mask and please others, I advise you to throw those beliefs in the garbage, ASAP. Guess what? People are going to have opinions, and some will even talk about you in an unflattering manner no matter how pleasant you aim to come across. That is life. You can't control what other people think and/or say about you, no matter *who* you are. Yep, even if you are like Jesus, people will talk, and you'll merely drain your energy trying to prove yourself. So, what should you do? Just *be*. Focus on being and bringing all of you to work. Again, your essence is diversity. Being yourself, mask-free, is freeing within itself. It can also tremendously reduce your stress. And although everyone may not have a taste for what you are bringing to the table, there will be people who do, so it's still important that you serve what you have and to be who you are.

When you aren't your authentic self, the company loses an opportunity to learn from you—i.e., your perspective and ideas. Your background has led you to this point, and because of it, you have profound knowledge, a new approach, and fresh strategies. Why suppress this?

We'll dive deeper into this in another chapter. For now, how do you see yourself in the workplace? Do you stand out? If so, how and where? Do you know the value you're adding to the team and company? Again, you're there for a reason.

Knowing that you are both on the menu and are the table is about knowing your worth and value. To survive in corporate, it is essential that you know your worth. In fact, to thrive and/or survive *anything* in this life, it is important for you to also know your value. You don't need a job, team, performance review, or manager to validate you. Let me repeat that. *You don't need a job, organization, performance review, or manager to authenticate you.* Don't get me wrong: Positive affirmations and feed-back are helpful and necessary to stimulate growth, but knowing who you are, what you deserve, and the value you add is most important. Knowing your worth is the best defense mechanism to offset disappointment.

Woosah, in its essence, is not only a survival guide, but also a reminder of your core and what you deserve, which is a peace of mind. You, my sista, have been fearfully and wonderfully made by a Creator who loves you too much to have you out there living life just to go to work, pay bills, fill your calendar with tasks, become stressed, and then die. You are created for so much more. You have a very distinct contribution to this planet, life, and even the workplace.

Your presence in the workplace is necessary, vital, and critical to the success of yourself and others. I believe that when we become who we're created to be, others are also able to become who they were designed to be. I want you to win, but I also want those connected to you to also win. It's a win-win for everyone. Why? Because this pushes humanity and those around you receive the *best* you. I like to call this version of you "the inspired you." And, guess what? The "inspired you" doesn't take crap. She also believes in herself and kicks butt. She walks in her truth, subsequently permitting others to walk in theirs.

So, despite the disheartening stats and uneven playing field, take a moment to reflect on everything that has led you to this point in your career. Think about the hardships, long hours, and even longer nights, sacrifices, successes, failures, and adversities. The good news is that you are here right now, so that means you got through them. You can process and reflect on what you are reading in this book. In other words, whatever hardships you are currently going through will eventually become a distant memory of reflection as well. Let me ask you this: If you could go back ten years, what advice would you give yourself? Think about that for a second and then jot the answer down below.

If I could go back ten years, what advice would I give myself?

_____

_____

_____

_____

_____

_____

_____

_____

_____

Guess what? You can use the same advice you would have given yourself ten years ago *now!* Believe it or not, it is still applicable even after all this time. Understand that nothing lasts forever, so you will persevere through hard times. I believe every obstacle is an opportunity to be groomed into who and what we're supposed to be, even when it's painfully harsh, and especially when it's tough. Obstacles provide us with tools for our tool kits—tools that we would not have if we hadn't struggled at some point in time.

Think in terms of video games—after you beat a hard level or beat the villain, you gain an extra life, an extra weapon, or advancement in some capacity. This is true in real life, as well. Every easy and difficult level is preparation for your next move. The trick is to be attentive during the process. You can't afford to miss a lesson or opportunity to grow. Maybe the obstacle is intended to refine your voice, perspective, fight, and capacity. Perhaps the intention is for you to become a positive light to others and contribute to their success. You and only you can accomplish this task. Adversities test who we say we are.

So give yourself credit for the adversities through which you have persevered. I'm sure you're handling life like a pro, doing the best you can with what you have been given. You deserve recognition! As women, we don't pat ourselves on our backs enough. It's easier to focus on what we did wrong, what's going wrong, and what we wish we had done. Stop it! It's high time we switched our focus to what we did right, what's going well, and what we are actually doing instead. It's time we focus on the value that we bring from (to revert to my kitchen analogy) being on the menu and being the table. It's also time we rid ourselves of this "strong black woman" ideology. She's exhausting! You don't have to be strong all the time. Sis, there is power in your weakness and vulnerability. Weakness and vulnerabilities point to humility, and they invite God to step in and help.

Life is cruel enough without us putting extra pressure on ourselves. The worst thing we can do is add to this by having a negative and toxic "strong black woman" mindset. Therefore, I encourage you to celebrate yourself. You have full permission be. Now, this doesn't mean you shouldn't work with a spirit of excellence. But it does mean you should let go of trying to control outcomes and doing everything solo. Furthermore, I encourage you to change your perspective. You've gotten this far for a reason.

I'm sure I don't have to remind you of the millions of qualified, yet unemployed people struggling to make ends meet and searching for work. Don't forget to be grateful! Expressing gratitude is gravely essential, but so are your feelings, and what you may have experienced in the past or what you are experiencing now. Your feelings are real and valid, but there *must* be a balance. Before mastering any environment, you first *must* master yourself—i.e., your mindset, your qualities and talents, and your place on the menu and you being the table. Remember, the "table" is synonymous with your unique contributions and ability to create opportunities. Repeat after me: "I am on the menu *and* I am the table! If I wasn't, I would not be here." You are valuable and an asset, so make the most of it!

In my workplace experience, there were times when I felt defeated from constantly being bossed around, undermined, discriminated against, disrespected, and even yelled at. There were times where my hostile environment caused me to question my own intelligence and morals. There were also moments where I should have spoken up, but didn't have my voice yet...

At times, the corporate world felt like a plantation that was run by cutthroat and brutal slave masters. Think about it; most corporate environments focus solely on performance and the bottom line, even at the expense of their employees. Many times, their response to objections is, "It's just the way we do things..." So, you either get with the program (i.e., abide by the rules, support the "bottom line") or get to stepping. There's little to no respect for people, humanity, sincerity, empathy, or even compassion. It's just the nature of the beast, I suppose. That is why understanding that *you* are on the menu is so vital. It is imperative that you separate your work from your life. Don't allow titles to define who you are. In my opinion, people who allow titles to define them are shallow and sad.

Who are you outside of work? If you're a jerk at work, does this mean you are one in your personal life as well? How tragic to live life exclusively for "the Man" and his bottom line. I've witnessed people bashing each other, recklessly tossing each other under the bus, gossiping all the time, and putting on fake smiles and pretending to care about people while voicing pleasantries like, "How was your weekend?" and "How are your kids?" It's all part of the game. It's putting on an act and playing the role—just long enough to get what he or she needs from you.

"So, what's the problem? It's just business," some might say. Yes, it's "business," but since you will spend roughly one-third of your life at work, you will need to feel valued and comfortable being there.

So, why is it so important for women of color to own the idea of being the table?

Well, according to the 2017 and 2018 "Women in Workplace" studies, white women typically have a better experience at the workplace than women of color, and especially black women. According to researchers, black women have the worst experiences at work, due to the factors that I mentioned in Chapter Two (unconscious biases, racism, and discrimination).

Results also indicated that women of color are also remarkably underrepresented, and less likely to receive support from their managers, be promoted in leadership roles, and are more likely to face racial discrimination on a regular basis. According to the US Census Bureau (2019), a white woman who works full time earns about $0.80 for every dollar earned by white men, while a black woman who works full time only earns about $0.67. This means that women of color not only face biases, but are also underpaid and rarely promoted. Even if they've had more education than men, corporate women in general are still disproportionate. But this issue is even more prevalent and particularly ominous for black women.

And because we are the most underrepresented group in corporate, we tend to experience the most challenges. Now, imagine being the *only* on your team (raises hand). Although many companies are making strides to increase diversity and inclusion at the workplace, diversity and inclusion alone aren't enough to adequately address the magnitude of issues black and brown women face. Therefore, we *must* disrupt, speak up, be ourselves, share our ideas, force the issue, and hold our employers accountable for anything that presents a threat to our growth.

> **"Diversity is being invited to the party; inclusion is being asked to dance."**
> —Verna Myers

Leslie Hunter-Gadsden, a contributor on nextavenue.org, highlighted studies done by LeanIn.Org and McKinsey & Co. Both studies echoed disturbing treatment of black women in the workplace. Alexis Krivkovich, the managing partner of McKinsey's Silicon Valley and cofounder of the partnership with Leanin.Org and McKinsey, began the study in 2015. She is also one of the co-authors of *Women in the Workplace*. Krivkovich reported that the impact of being an "only" is a phenomenon that affects approximately 20% of all women, and 40% of women of color specifically. As a result, Krivkovich found that women of color feel uniquely alone, partly due to having to represent the entire race, rather than being looked at as individuals.

Additionally, Krivkovich found that people who describe themselves as being an "only" also report experiencing more microaggressions in the workplace and more instances of their decision-making skills being questioned than non-minorities. In fact, according to the survey, approximately 51% of female "onlys" reported that they had to provide more evidence of their competence than others (Leslie Hunter-Gadsden, 2018).

I believe this is why many women, like myself, have remained silent. Challenges associated with speaking up and the extra steps to prove ourselves is *exhausting*. However, silence is dangerous. It's the reason nothing changes, people depart, and growth is stalled. It's articles, stats, surveys, and studies like the one listed above that support the need for minorities to know their value. Despite harsh discriminatory realities, knowing who you are provides peace of mind. Peace of mind is *invaluable*. When you have a good grasp of who you are and how much you're worth, these harsh realities cannot strip you of your value and authentic essence.

For example, that $20 bill you accidentally washed in your jeans pocket doesn't change its value after it has been washed. It may have gotten wet, folded, balled up, or torn in the washing and drying process, but its value hasn't changed, despite the circumstances. It's still twenty dollars. So, just as crazy work circumstances may take you to the kitchen, roast you in the fire, and attempt to serve you for dinner, you are still who you are, and you are still on the menu. So, why not give others a *real* taste of you?

If you walk away with your dignity intact, you can walk away with your head held high. More specifically, you can walk into a space knowing you can't be robbed of the one thing that is priceless—your peace. Sometimes it takes spreading your wings to obtain this peace. Some environments won't change so you'll need to have the courage to choose you. For now, while you are on the menu, you have an opportunity to serve what you have.

Let's take a quick inventory of exactly what you're serving.

List your top strengths (i.e., work examples where you naturally demonstrated these strengths):

1.

2.

3.

List what you're serving (i.e., your "uniqueness" and what sets you apart from others):

1.

2.

3.

List what you love about yourself.

1.

2.

3.

Great! See, you got this! Now, I would like for you to study, embrace, and own everything you just listed above. Practice saying your answers aloud. Be confident and sell yourself! Highlight your strengths and skills, and *believe* that the diversity you bring to the table is incomparable. In other words, get in a positive headspace! Get rid of any negative external factors that may be affecting your ability to think and see yourself clearly.

This mindset shift is one of your most important leverages for surviving and conquering the corporate world. Knowing your uniqueness, strengths, and what you love about yourself can also change how others perceive you. How? Well, you will start to radiate a high level of positive energy, and "unbotheredness" (yes, I made this word up). It's this "unbotheredness" that forces others to respect you as you are. "Unbotheredness" means that you are unshakeable and fine either way, that you're…unbothered. It is a high level of contentment and confidence. Attaining this type of confidence can help you ask for pay raises, seek promotions, call out injustices, pitch projects, and/or ask for feedback. It is also this level of self-assuredness that provides you with the courage to express disagreement and the assertiveness to declare you've had enough when that time comes. You are and have everything you need. It is *oozing* out of your being and uniqueness.

Sis, you are definitely on the menu and are the table, so let them take a seat and experience a side of you that they've never tasted.

CHAPTER FOUR

IDENTIFYING TOXICITY AND TAKING ACTION!

Over the course of my professional career, I've had the privilege of working for multiple companies in different departments, capacities and on a variety of teams. Each opportunity provided a level of exposure to intricate aspects of the business. The variety allowed me a chance to interact with talented people from all walks of life. While a good deal of my experience was positive and rewarding, there were countless challenges. Like most things, you have to take the good with the bad. But what if the "bad" becomes too much? This was my story at many points. The bad made it overwhelmingly difficult to remain in a positive headspace. Some cultures were flat out stressful and toxic! Much of the toxicity stemmed from unprofessional, dishonest and micromanaging leadership, favoritism, cliquishness, poor management, and unbridled gossip. I can't speak for each entire company, but certainly on behalf of my experiences and those of many of my colleagues as well.

Working in a fast-paced, ratings-, deadline-, and head-line-driven industry only made matters worse. I don't need to tell you how difficult it is to juggle work stress and toxicity, much less processing or navigating it. I mean, we need our jobs, benefits, and compensation, right? But at what cost? Isn't peace priceless? Shouldn't the insti-gators, trash bosses, enablers, slackers, and hellraisers in the workplace be let go? Wouldn't it be nice if things were just that simple? Why can't people just show up to work with sense and integrity, be unbiased, work hard, be professional and execute efficiently?

My granny would say, "That's too much like right!"

Maybe it really is too much like right, because likely this won't happen. I mentioned in the intro the value and importance of creating and sustaining a healthy work culture. Healthy work cultures are produced by effective leadership and maintained by great employees. Effective leaders are effective coaches who help weed out toxicity. People will be people (whom we can't control). I get that; however, constantly "checking" and "correcting" toxicity in the work culture *must* be a priority. Period.

Remember, it's usually the work atmosphere/culture and environment that *forces* great workers too quit, elevates their blood pressure, and drives them to happy hours or hour-long sessions on therapy couches. How many people do you think would be willing to take a pay cut in exchange for a healthier and more engaging work environment? Understand that the work environment and culture is *queen.*

Don't get me wrong, I get that it's hard to speak up publicly, especially in reference to leadership and unhealthy work cultures. In fact, there's a real fear of speaking up at work. Heck, there's a real fear of speaking up *anywhere,* despite us understanding how dangerous silence can be. Truthfully, writing this book was occasionally uncomfortable. More specifically, speaking my truth was difficult at times, but it it's necessary for my growth. I'm convinced that the main reason nothing changes is because of people's silence and lack of accountability. As a result, the status quo remains the same, people depart (or escape), and growth never happens. No one wants to be blackballed or blacklisted—I get that, too. I mean… who *wants* to be hated by colleagues and/or considered a "whistleblower?" No one.

Still, you must speak up at some point or risk suffering in silence or be forced to exit stage left. Difficult conversations are a part of growth. Personally, I would rather be hated for speaking up or standing up for something I believe, than live my life in silence. Now, I can understand staying quiet, if I was a bona fide troublemaker, unreliable, and unbelievable—or if I had an HR rap sheet as long as a CVS receipt. But I don't…In fact, I can honestly say that *every* job (including my first job at age 16), and *every* performance review has been nothing short of exemplary. My work ethic, reputation, and resume are extremely important to me. Yours should be equally as important to you.

I believe a person's reputation speaks volumes in both their personal and professional life. Is there room for me to grow? Absolutely! That is why I am an advocate for professional and personal development—an agent for change. I care about equity and I care about people. So how can companies, nonprofit organizations, individuals, and businesses grow if they are unwilling to receive important feedback, address pressing issues, and expose cancerous behaviors? Simply put, they can't.

My hope is that I can help you identify the toxicity in your work environment and provide realistic strategies to circumvent it. So, what makes a work environment toxic? I'm glad you asked. I don't have all the answers, but listed below are a couple of ideas and questions to get us started. I believe the answer lies in your response to the text below.

Working in a toxic environment with toxic people can look like the following:

1. Ineffective Leadership and Management

Ever had a manager, supervisor or director that lacked clarity and direction or the ability to set realistic expectations? What about the lazy, clueless, lackadaisical, passive-aggressive, dishonest one who avoids conflict? Characteristics, behaviors and workstyles like these from the person in charge is tumorous to a healthy work culture.

Each of the 12 women I spoke with expressed distrust of management because they didn't believe minorities were capable of successfully performing their job duties. At least, these were their observations of management treating them as such, myself included. Managers have a professional duty to keep things confidential and to govern justly, unbiasedly, and professionally. But the harsh truth is that some people just aren't cut out to be effective leaders.

True leaders are emotionally intelligent. They are born to serve others, regardless of gender or race. However, sometimes the wrong people end up in leadership roles—for the *wrong* reasons. These wrong people then begin managing others and making wrong executive decisions when it comes to you and your career. These individuals should have never been granted a leadership position in the first place. But yet there they are—and there *you* are.

Ineffective leaders struggle with things like professionalism, composure, and governing in a responsible and assertive way. Strong leaders do not major in the minor, and they're able to separate personal feelings from business.

Leadership is not a position; it's a posture.

Effective leaders understand the difference between being friendly and being friends. I had a manager who wanted to be friends (bad)…at least, she pretended to. She was a kind person, but a terrible leader. She had little-to-no professional acumen, and because of this she should have never been hired for a leadership position. She engaged in work gossip and had a habit of sharing unsolicited personal information about the team with me and others. The funny part is that I don't believe she saw anything wrong with her actions. That behavior, chile… she couldn't have realized how unprofessional she was being. The woman was extremely nosy, often prying and asking about my dating life and other personal tidbits. I gave her vague, general answers…never anything I didn't want repeated.

At times, I figured maybe she was just trying to make me feel welcomed, because I was the *only* person of color in my area. Sadly, she failed and was insulting instead. She was micro-aggressive and frequently made insensitive comments. Her fruitless efforts to connect with me missed the mark every single time. The thing that really made me cringe was when she referred to her direct reports as "friends" and "sisters." Fix it, Jesus! Her personal relationships with employees *clouded* her ability to manage the team without biases. In desperate attempts to get others to like her, she tended to be tempered and insecure. After a while, it became a nightmare to work with her.

Being supervised by an ineffective leader while working alongside her produced much stress for me; I found it overwhelming. Seriously, I could write an entire book just about my experiences working in that department and under that particular supervisor. The book would be titled *But, Do You Like Me?: A Guide to Ineffective Leadership*. At the same time, I had to give it to her, for she exercised her privilege well. She often bragged about how she had only had one job working at McDonald's prior to working for the company. She recalls how she worked her way up from multiple departments, finally storming her way into a director's office demanding a promotion. She walked out a manager (with no management experience) defeating other more-educated and experienced black women on her team (who were all hired at the same time). Must be nice. I know no person of color who is able to do that.

Like many other underqualified managers, I assume she was promoted because of favoritism, privilege and office politics. Her race and ability to play the game with the right powerful people helped her win (at least for the moment). Keep in mind, it's people like her who are gatekeepers of minority promotions. Her lack of professionalism alone should've garnered denial. If she were a person of color, she wouldn't be in that position with that behavior. #facts

What is your manager's style like? Does it work for you? What are three things you would change about your manager? Write them down. This may be good content for your next one-on-one, if communicated tactfully.

_____

_____

_____

_____

_____

_____

‗‗
‗‗
‗‗
‗‗

2. Silos & Hesitant Collaborations

Deep dread stemming from cultural differences, different opinions and a lack of diversified teams are often root causes for silos and hesitant collaborations for women of color. Cliques and management's neglect in fostering collaborative cultures is a prevalent cause as well. It's the anxiety produced in the fear of being misunderstood and undermined, making the desire of working solo more appeasing. By the time we're done explaining, setting the stage, strategizing, disarming and highlighting our credibility we're too exhausted to begin collaborating.

Now, this isn't the case for every woman of color of course, I get it. But this is certainly common. The additional mental and emotional work (added as taxes) to the actual task can be overwhelming. While all these factors hold validity they can also contribute to a more toxic environment. What is the solution? I would say request smaller teams; ask your supervisor to be intentional with diversifying teams. Request to have team leads appointed, and for them to be coached prior. You can also suggest different content management and communication platforms. Lastly, icebreakers and setting ground rules for collaborations are helpful.

3. Conniving Behaviors & Toxic People

Conniving behaviors and toxic people are present in the workplace far too often. THESE PEOPLE ARE UNHAPPY! Their behaviors and true natures tend to be covertly masked by warm smiles and fake positive energy. Beware! They'll become your "friend" and ask about your family and/or your time off, while creating messy and hurtful "narratives" about all the information they receive from you. They'll send out unnecessary petty emails about you (issues that could have been a private conversation between the two of you), while cc'ing and bcc'ing management on it. Give me a break! Many of these personality types are similar to those of the "Karen and Kevin" persona. Who are Karen and Kevin and what is this persona? I'm glad you asked. Well they aren't just single people but a cross between white privilege, entitlement, self-appointed policing, and simply harassing behaviors. This persona is demanding beyond the scope of what's necessary and or reasonable at the expense of others, specifically black people.

Culturally, they are the ones obsessed with calling the cops on innocent black and brown people due to his/her own displeasure in life. In other words, this person has no business or personal life so they engulf themselves in yours. Amy Cooper from the Central Park bird-watching incident is certainly a Karen. Karen and Kevin are highly infiltrated in the workplace and specifically in the corporate culture. They are decision makers and relentless in attempts to tear down and minimize black and brown people to make themselves feel good.

People like this conspire to trip others up and get them reprimanded, written up or even fired. As self-appointed watchdogs, they wait for trouble and then they pounce on it. Why do they do this, you ask? Because they are pessimistic and sad. They hate to see people of color win, happy or simply enjoy life. They're the ones who are never satisfied and *always* complaining about something. Their energy and dispositions are atrocious! Chile, these people will *drain* you! The takeaway? These are vindictive people who feed off of drama and chaos. So, do yourself a favor and avoid interactions when you see them coming—or at the very least, ignore them, especially if they're not your superior.

I'd be lying if I said I didn't sit alongside many of these personality types during my time in corporate. I believe *some* of my colleagues thrived off drama. Some were also impulsive, and as a result couldn't help their behaviors. Those were the ones who even talked about their own friends behind their backs. Jealousy was another factor; I believe some were jealous and others just miserable, and as we all know, misery loves company. In fact, I once tragically witnessed a colleague (a white woman) stoop to the deplorable low of paying for a background check on another colleague (a black woman) after searching her on the web and finding a mugshot. Like, why was she Googling this woman in the first place? Sadly, the background check came back with damning information from the colleague's past—information that she delighted in sharing with me and several other colleagues.

If that wasn't bad enough—after she finished gossiping about it to other colleagues, she went to management with her findings. Yes, you heard right. One of my white colleagues stalked a black colleague (whom she didn't like, which you've probably already guessed) found negative information, paid for a background check, and shared the results with management (after making sure everyone else in the department knew about the woman's criminal past). Shortly after, the black woman was fired. Watching it unfold was both depressing and horrifying. I couldn't believe that happened, so I started distancing myself from that colleague. I don't have a criminal background or anything to hide, but it was anxiety-provoking to witness, nonetheless. I wish I could have spoken up just to get it off my chest, but wasn't sure with whom I could responsibly share my feelings. I certainly didn't want my name mixed up in this unfortunate situation, and by confiding my feelings about the matter, it possibly could have done more harm.

The moral of the story is to watch your back, and if you witness people gossiping about others or exhibiting conniving/toxic behaviors toward others, they *will* do it to you. Scratch that—they *are* doing it to you, as we speak, behind your back. Keep things really brief and cordial with these individuals.

Have you observed toxic people/behaviors from people on your team? If so, list them. These are the people you want to stay away from whenever possible, keep boundaries between them

and you, and limit your conversations to the business at hand.

---

4. Oppressive GOSSIP Cultures

No one is safe in this type of culture. More specifically, if colleagues deliberately engage in sharing negative opinions of others, they ultimately have no filter, loyalty, or concern as to how this gossip may harm someone else. In other words, they are perfectly OK with creating the venom and freely spewing it onto others. And that is a problem. Gossip distorts perceptions, confidence, morale, and peace. It hurts, divides, and destroys the harmony needed to effectively work together.

If you can't say anything nice…don't say anything at all.

Even if you don't indulge in gossip yourself, just being in its vicinity is toxic. The negative energy associated with gossiping is transferable. It seeps into your pores, just like secondhand smoke. You can't control what comes out of people's mouths, but you *can* control what you allow in your space. You have the power to remove yourself from negative situations. But what if you're stuck on a team or project with a Gossiping Gloria type? The success of the project is threatened if Gossiping Gloria, instead of listening or contributing to ideas, is instead telling the person next to her about who was crying in the ladies room, or who she saw going to lunch together. You can simply ask her to stop and stay on task.

I know, I know, that's a tough situation. Speaking up could possibly get you that "who-does-she-think-she-is" look. You also may be viewed as an elitist. I get it, but you still should do it. Girl, protect your peace! Think about it like this…you're probably well aware of who the "chat-terboxes" are. So, whenever possible, stay away from them. Why? Because you can't afford to be associated with them. Your name and reputation are too important. Remember the old expression about being judged by the company you keep? Running in those circles can and will be disastrous. And, if you hang with people who spread gossip, you may be held responsible if something happens, simply because your name is associated with theirs. Do you see how that works?

One of the twelve women I interviewed said, "Trust me—I sat grudgingly at the gossip lunch table (out of obligation) one too many times. I felt indebted because I didn't want to seem unapproachable. The team would also 'jokingly' make sarcastic remarks about me not eating with them. And, being the only black woman on that team, the pressure was on. So, I would have 'lunch' with the girls. Lunch really consisted of fresh off-the-press gossip. Usually, I sat in silence, occasionally nodding or scrolling on my phone. The times that I would contribute,

I intentionally said something unrelated or optimistic. Still, I frequently walked away feeling like crap."

Don't do this, Sis. Muster your courage and aim to make a bigger difference. Say to the gossiper, "Please stop. I don't need to hear or know this." You can also redirect the conversation by asking if the gossiper has reached out to the person or persons being discussed. Change the subject, or highlight something positive about the person of focus. Basically, either shut it down as soon as it starts, or remove yourself. Just get up and leave. If you do this often enough, they'll get the point and know not to involve you in their foolery. Setting the "I don't associate or participate in gossip" standard is an excellent way to thrive corporate. It's one less thing that you'll have to worry about. When you do this, you are setting up a boundary (we'll dive into boundaries later). Setting that standard and shutting down the gossip is critical.

Does anyone, anything, or any particular instance in this category come to mind? How have or how would you handle this behavior? Also, have you encountered any Karens or Kevins in your workspace?

_____

_____

_____

_____

_____

_____

_____

5. Cliques, Discrimination, Privilege, Nepotism, & Favoritism

This can be tough to witness, especially if you're on the other end of the inclusion spectrum. It's painful watching underqualified individuals advance ahead of you, receive preferential treatment and perks (not available to everyone), and earn more than you because of their race and/or who they know. We have all witnessed this in some capacity. And if you haven't, maybe you were the victim. It's painful. Period. No, actually, it's beyond painful—it's infuriating and disgusting. I have personally witnessed and been impacted by cliquish behaviors, unconscious and deliberate biases, privilege, nepotism, and favoritism on more than a few occasions.

For example, let's discuss a young lady who we'll call Black Woman X. She works as an assistant in the executive suite of Company Y. Black Woman X is an "only," working alongside three white women and four senior level white male executives. Each woman supports a male executive. This position not only allows the women to work closely with executives, it also gives them opportunities to carefully observe the company's decision-makers and influencers in action.

However, Black Woman X's experience is different than that of her white colleagues—who, by the way, received red carpet treatment. Black Woman X has witnessed her colleagues collect continuous overtime, weekly expensed lunches, opportunities to travel, extra bonuses, early dismissals, and even time out of the office to get their hair and nails done. Yes, you read right. These women were collecting their salaries while at the salon. It's a perk that Black Woman X could only imagine. As a matter of fact, she's usually left to cover the phones and the workloads while her colleagues are away.

We're not talking about normal office shenanigans. These women are permitted to do as they please because of their relationships with their respective bosses. So, naturally, the favoritism in this department is offensive to Black Woman X. You're probably wondering why Black Woman X hasn't said anything. Well, the first issue is where she sits and who she supports. Because these are senior level executives, the entire building (including HR) essentially works with them in some capacity. So, speaking up would be an uphill battle and likely cause unwanted tension.

Besides, other colleagues have questioned management's judgement in the presence of Black Woman X and those coworkers. They've noticed times when Black Woman X was the only one present and working. In these instances, Black Woman X observed her coworkers pretend to be clueless when others questioned their actions. They knew how to lay it on thick, pretending not to know what the others were talking about. Black Woman X also knew that speaking up would require her to jump through hoops to provide detailed examples, and the thought of defending herself is exhausting. Saturated in privilege, her colleagues are convinced their super friendly and approachable demeanors are great covers to mask their conduct. And, because Black Woman X hasn't called them out on anything, they think she's oblivious. The overt favoritism is problematic for a variety of reasons, the first being that the company loses when employees take advantage and aren't actively engaged at work. Then there's the cliquish element to this entire fiasco. Not only is Black Woman X offended, but others in the department have observed these behaviors as well. Sadly, this clique is particularly influential in management's decisions.

The women working with Black Woman X play the game well, so it favors them.

As a woman of color, imagine telling your white boss that you're going to get your hair braided or nail polish changed, and you'll be back in a couple of hours. Are you shaking your head or laughing yet? Yeah, so am I. Even if you had the gall to say that to your boss, as a woman of color, can you imagine what he or she would say? Probably something like, "Absolutely not. You need to handle personal matters on your own time—not the company's."

It's always crazy to me when I hear some of the things people are comfortable doing on their jobs. Think of all the people who embezzle money, forge time-off, and do other illegal stuff that make running personal errands on company time—unethical but not illegal—look almost innocent—it's insane.

I believe most of it is a blatant abuse of power and privilege. It's what causes some people to feel like they are invincible. I'm not suggesting that Black Woman X witnessed these extremes, but an abuse of power is an abuse of power. Period. These are the types of work cultures (displaying favoritism, privilege, and nepotism) that foster these types of aversive behaviors. I neglected to mention that Black Woman X's (and the women she worked with) boss's husband was a close friend to one of the senior level white male executives on the floor who her boss reported to. Confusing, right? Black Woman X expressed how everyone appeared to be in cahoots due to all the personal relationships. So there was certainly no oversight, regulation, accountability, or fairness.

The Overlooked Talented Trio

I observed three extremely qualified women of color get passed over for promotions. Sadly, I witnessed this unfold before my very eyes and knew each woman personally. After much examination, I realized that the majority of the hiring and promotions in my department were influenced through a small clique of white male leaders (similar to Black Woman X's story).

Actually, my department had a *reputation* for not promoting people of color. In fact, it often went like this: A black woman fills in as an alternate in an open position until a permanent replacement can be hired. In the interim, she learns and masters the job. She grows to like it and learns that it pays more, so when it posts she interviews for it.

She thinks, *Surely, I will get it because I was granted an interview and I've been doing this work a while.* But does she get the job? *No.* She is not only passed over for the job that she has already proven she is qualified for, but she's asked to "train" the new hire—even though she was an ideal candidate. Seriously? Yes, seriously. I've watched this happen more than once.

Each time, a non-minority person with no experience was either promoted or hired over the person of color with a ton of experience. And each time, the new hire had a personal connection to or association with upper management.

We also had two talented black veterans on the team, both with 20+ years of tenure with the company. They had excellent reputations and impeccable work ethics, but were nonetheless passed over for promotions, losing out to less talented non-minorities. This type of blatant unfairness was flagrant within the department, and it doesn't take a rocket scientist to see the obvious.

Corporate leadership made it very clear through their actions that they're *not* in the business of promoting people of color. It was painfully evident to me and many of my colleagues that black people who *deserved* promotions did not receive them. And to make matters worse there were only two people of color in management and none in upper leadership in our entire department. So, not only did cliquish behavior, nepotism, and favoritism play out in the department, discrimination was also just as rampant.

Have you noticed any cliques, discrimination, privilege, nepotism, or favoritism at your job? Let's talk about it. Is this something you're willing to address? Jot it down.

_____

_____

_____

_____

_____

6. Health Changes

If your work environment is making you sick, depressed, and/or anxious, there is a problem! If you are chronically stressed, unnaturally introverted, or have a strong desire to avoid your colleagues *and* management, your work environment may be highly toxic, or you may be working with toxic people. If you experience sickness or anxiety when approaching your job's parking lot, or if you struggle to sleep at night because you are constantly worried about the rest of the work week—work is harming your wellbeing. And if you are ghastly afraid of missing an email, making a mistake, being reprimanded, dropping the ball, and/or missing deadlines, your health is most likely being negatively impacted by your work environment. This is too much control over your emotions.

Lastly, if you don't feel you can be yourself and/or you feel fatigued, sad, or disturbed by your environment because it drains your energy…something *must* give. Sis, listen to your body and pay close attention to your health. These are signs that your workplace is harmful to you. If you can relate to any of this, you are in a toxic environment!

So, my advice to you is to do something about this. Speak up. Take time off and regroup. Be sure to document anti-policy or inappropriate incidents, create an action plan, disrupt the drama. It may also be time to consider firing your employer. You are way too talented to retreat and not be your full self at work. I fired my employer because I had to. You *must* do what is best for you. Working in environments that conflict with your health can kill you, i.e., your spirit, confidence, essence, and even your physical body.

Let's say that you've identified your work environment as toxic, a gossip culture plagued by ineffective leadership, where nepotism, favoritism, and discrimination are the norm. What should you do? Below are some of my suggestions on what to do when you don't know what to do. *I only wish I knew then, what I know now.*

Toxic Environment Action Plan

- **Michelle Obama**

"Kill them with kindness." "When they go low, we go high!" High enough to poop on them. Just kidding! Seriously, this may be a bit challenging, but it will pay off. So be kind to everyone, especially the toxic people. Kill them with kindness, and when possible, go out of your way to serve them. These people may need your positive energy to balance them out. As long as you continue to be your authentic self, despite your environment, *they will not win.* Their problems and toxicity will not be able to affect you. Trust me, bad behavior will catch up with them (even if you're not around to see it).

- **Decide**

Is this environment right for you? You may love your job, but hate the environment. However, you'll need to think about whether you can be productive working under these challenging conditions.

Ask yourself the following questions:

> ➢ Is your work environment impacting your health? If so, how? Do what is best for you, but it's best to do *something.* Keep in mind that dismissing or ignoring roadblocks will not make them magically disappear.
> ➢ Do you believe that speaking up can or will help other people be treated more fairly? If so, why? In addition, do you think it is time to fire your boss? If so, why? If it's time to go, start updating your resume...like, *yesterday.*

Also, make sure your LinkedIn profile is up to date, create a couple of search agents, and sign up for job alerts from job search sites like Indeed.com or Monster.com. Be visible. See what is out there. Don't forget to also tap into your networks for potential job opportunities.

But if you *choose* to stay, see below.

- **Set Boundaries**

  Set boundaries and clarify what you will and will not engage in, allow, or tolerate. Train other people on how to treat you. Say no when your plate is full. At the end of the day, shut work off. Stop being always readily available. You are no slave to work. Understand that work should not have the power to impact other areas of your life. Set clear expectations and avoid sharing too many personal details with your colleagues. Your job is *not* the place for this. Don't feel obligated to play the game. We will talk more about boundaries in the next chapter. This is important because healthy boundaries are lifesavers.

- **Study Policy and Document *Everything***

  More specifically, document inappropriate incidents, behaviors, and policy conflicts. Keep a record of inappropriate requests from your boss and the times you were unfairly denied a legitimate request, witnessed favoritism, unfair treatment, racial slurs, insensitive jokes, dishonesty in leadership, abuse, and any other issues that are threatening your health and wellbeing. Include the date, time, and the names of anyone else who was present.

  Also, document your special accomplishments, like the times you went above and beyond what was required, when you saved the company money, or the new system approaches you created. Why should you do that? Because it will lead to a fantastic yearly performance review.

  These things, good and bad, should always be documented. Now, I'm not saying you should become a tattle-tale, but if you want to recall these occasions, it's nice to have a paper trail with specifics. You may not need to use these documents, but they are still vital to have. You may need them if you want to move up in the company, dispute write-ups, or support why you deserve a promotion or bonus. It's also good to have if you have to challenge a yearly performance review that fails to recognize your positive contributions.

I have kept—and used—documentation to prove my point, protect myself, or to file grievances in the past. I have made it a habit to document *every* noteworthy encounter I have had with a boss or colleague. Yes, it can be very tedious to do; however, bosses tend to get amnesia. Fortunately, my documentation has come in handy multiple times. It has been an easy resource that supports discrepancies. You can either handwrite the documents and place them in a folder or email them to your personal email address. You should also make a copy to keep at home.

In addition to including dates, times, names, and any witnesses who can corroborate your accounts, emailing documents to yourself will create a timestamp and shield you from accusations of creating these documents after the fact. Knowing and following corporate policy also adds a layer of protection. Let me rephrase this—it *should*. But just in case document *everything* (eye roll).

It is important to note, however, that in many cases, even if you provide written documentation, the powers that be may likely side with the company over you, so mentally prepare for that scenario. From my experience, I've learned many HR departments favor the protection of the company vs. the employees' comfort. Still, don't be afraid to stand on truth! This goes back to deciding if you want to continue your employment, especially if you work for a company that doesn't value its employees. Therefore, I believe in exhausting other options first, like speaking up and following protocol—even if these things do not change the environment.

When you speak up, it shows the powers that be that you are not afraid to use your voice…that you are going to stand up for what's right. Speaking up also supports those who will come after you, because your voice helped pave the way. Hopefully, you will come across as someone who is 100% committed to fostering a healthy work environment.

If you have to file a grievance, do it! Don't be intimidated. Force HR to do their jobs, even if you don't plan on staying, still file it. Think of the potential positive outcome. That is why I detailed the importance of documentation. Documentation is beneficial when filing a grievance. Be prepared to be on your A-game if you file one in the event of retaliation. Don't be naïve; filing grievances could invoke retaliation from management, colleagues, or employers. If this happens, simply document everything that feels retaliatory. If someone even looks at you cross-eyed, document that, too. Most companies have a retaliation policy, as some people sue their former employers, charging hostile work environments. However, be sure to protect yourself. Girl, you got this!

• **Who is in Charge?**

It is essential that you know who your HR representatives are. It is also important that you understand organizational charts so you know the chain of command, should you need to report a person or incident. Find out who reports to who, and as much of their backstory as you can. Knowing the critical players is essential if you plan to speak up. Seriously, unless your emotions are made of Teflon, choosing to stay in a toxic environment will eventually wear you down and force you to take action, perhaps walk off the job, perhaps have a meltdown. You'll want to avoid this at all costs.

I mean, why should you have to tolerate foolery when you can hold the fools accountable? Your voice may pave the way for something epic. What if Rosa Parks just got up and moved to the back of the bus? What if Harriet Tubman never went back South to lead more slaves to freedom after her first successful escape? Our ancestors were resilient women, and so are we. It's important to know the right people to talk to. Everyone has a boss, so don't become discouraged and start thinking you can't reach out to anyone, because that simply isn't true. But first, you will need to research the chain of command. You may also want to cc others on your emails for accountability purposes. Some companies also offer anonymous hotlines for reporting workplace issues.

But what if you feel uncomfortable reporting issues? What if you're threatened? In that case, request anonymity. Let's say your name gets leaked anyway. So what? You hold the power. Cross-reference your company's retaliation policy, and research the EEOC's role in work-place complaints. Speak with a labor attorney. Companies are often eager to avoid negative publicity and will offer you the support you deserve. They don't want lawsuits. And, if you need to there is always social media to help draw attention and garner support. Overall, you'll need to decide if you want to stay. If so, consider transferring to a different team or department.

- **Self-Care**

Self-care is often reduced to this pseudo notion of relaxation, like massages, napping, or getting a manicure. While relaxation can be and is a part of self-care, it's not the end-all. Proper self-care is identifying your needs, communicating them, and advocating for yourself until they're met! Self-care on the job is really about setting solid boundaries. However, from a relaxation and brain-clearing standpoint, it can take the form of a variety of activities, like watching your favorite television show while you eat lunch or taking a nap in your car during breaks. Take a stroll around the building, take a couple of three-to eight-minute breaks by walking away from your desk, ask to work remotely from your home, listen to uplifting music/podcast (if not disruptive to your concentration), and/or write a transition out plan. Technically, the transition out plan should be done on your own time but you get the picture ☺. You can also re-read the positive affirmations you have posted around your workspace. If you don't have any, visit my website, www.rahkalshelton.com

(and flip to the end of this book and use those). All these self-care activities can keep you motivated and focused.

Lord knows I have used all of these strategies at my previous jobs, and they were extremely helpful—until it was time for me to leave. Is there any way to request a lateral transfer to another team or task? If not, form a good relationship with a couple of your colleagues and speak your truth. Share what you are thinking and feeling with them. Having a trusted tribe at work is essential to surviving corporate. We will dive deeper into the importance of having a community at work later.

Let's talk:

Has work impacted your health lately (good or bad)?

_____

_____

_____

_____

_____

_____

_____

_____

_____

_____

_____

_____

_____

_____

When are you most excited, feeling valued and like you're making contributions?

_____
_____
_____
_____
_____

How do you like to be managed? Have you ever needed to manage up (making your boss's job easier by **managing** your manager)?

_____
_____
_____
_____
_____

When was the last time you've experienced work-related anxiety or stress? What triggered this?

_____
_____
_____
_____

What are your stress coping mechanisms? How do you de-stress at work?

_____
_____
_____
_____

Is it time to fire your employer? List the pros and cons of staying where you are.

_____

_____

_____

_____

_____

These are all vital factors to explore, consider, and know. You got this! For additional exercises and activities around self-care and identifying toxicity, be sure to grab your copy of the _Woosah Workplace Peace Workbook & Journal_ for women of color at www.rahkalshelton.com/woosah.

CHAPTER FIVE

MANAGING STRESS!

It would be irresponsible to only discuss work-related stress in this chapter. Although *Woosah* predominantly focuses on the workplace, stress is still stress, regardless of what triggers it. Let's talk about work-related stress— first. Work stress comes in different forms, shapes, situations, projects, encounters, and even people. Yes, *people*. In fact, for some, just hearing a person's name can trigger stress and anxiety.

In other words, these individuals are *always* stressed— causing the stress, witnessing it, or experiencing it. Is your boss or manager stressed or stressful? Does he or she ineffectively lead or delegate tasks poorly? What are some negative impacts of this ineffectiveness in the workplace?

Work-related stress stems from the following:

1. Discrimination & Microaggressions

We spoke about some of this in chapter 2. I'll venture to say that discrimination, racism, and micro-aggressions are among the top stressors for women of color in the workplace. We all know what it's like to work in stressful situations and environments that are not conducive to our livelihoods, health, and personal goals. We also understand that stress kills literally and figuratively. For women of color, these nuances can expedite a decline in health, and there is a difference between everyday work stress and racial stress.

For example, microaggressive insults communicate negative attitudes toward black and brown people. These dangerous workplace assaults foster deeper divides and an inability to see the humanity in each other. My granny would summarize microaggressions in this phrase: "White people like to throw rocks and hide they hands."

While grammatically incorrect, you gotta love that raw elderly candor! Her phrase is accurate and spot-on for many of my experiences and the women I interviewed. The politically correct language and examples are:

Microassaults: This is when a person intentionally behaves in a discriminatory way while not intending to be offensive. An example is telling a racist joke, then saying, "I was just joking."

Microinsults: This is a comment or action that is unintentionally discriminatory. For example, saying to an Indian doctor, "Your people must be so proud."

Microinvalidations: This is when a person's comment invalidates or undermines the experiences of a marginalized group. For example, a white colleague telling a black colleague, "Everything was fine until George Floyd died," or, "Racism does not exist in today's society" (PS: All real examples. SMH).

Discrimination is an entirely different type of stress beast because it can be covert, and we don't always know that it's happening, sometimes until after the fact. There is dread associated with the need to filter through race to determine if we're being singled out, unfairly compensated, overlooked, underpromoted, or targeted. Characteristics like these are the DNA of toxic environments.

We talked about these environments in the previous chapter. However, to make it plain, working in a toxic environment is much bigger than just having a bad (stress-filled) day or being displeased with coming to work. Toxic environments are the culprits for stress. These environments will impact your health (mentally, physically, or emotionally). And for many women of color, discrimination and microaggressive behaviors are embedded in these environments, thus producing more stress.

2. Low Wages

Seriously, who wants to work at a company that underpays him or her, but still expects him or her to perform at a high level with accuracy, while continually being asked for more, more, and more? In previous chapters, we talked about toxic people, but there is a difference between toxic people and stressful people. Toxic environments and people are definitely stressful; however, just because a task is stressful doesn't mean it's toxic. Wait...*what?* I know this probably sounds weird, but hear me out...

Don't you know people who love their job and love their team, but who are also extremely stressed because of their job or team? The truth is, a job or team doesn't have to be toxic to be stressful. It's possible to love your job, have a great team and workplace, but still feel stressed. While some people become stressed because of toxic work environments and people, others become stressed because of insane demands and heavy work-loads, often assigned by stressful people and bosses who are governing in ways that cause even more stress.

3. Heavy Workloads

Heavy workloads can leave people feeling stretched too thin and overwhelmed. These workloads can also trigger anxiety and a fear of not finishing tasks by deadline. In turn, this fear of not completing tasks in a timely manner creates worry of losing one's job. Those who experience this type of stress do whatever they have to do to complete tasks, even if it means skipping lunch, coming to work early, staying late, and/or working off the clock.

This can be extremely detrimental to our families, personal lives, and health, yet we still do it. But there are no gold stars or ribbons waiting for us, and there is definitely no extra compensation for our efforts. Great work is rewarded with more work. I had to learn to leave some tasks for the next day, especially if it was time for me to get off. Rome wasn't built in a day, right? So, there will be times when you won't be able to finish all of your tasks in a day. Do you think your supervisor will wait with you at the ER after you become ill from all the stress you're under? Nope. So, take care of yourself.

4. Little to No Acknowledgment, Growth *or* Professional Development

This is critical for me, and I'm sure it's a priority for many of you, as well. And if it isn't...it *should* be. A wise person is *always* pondering their next move and taking actions that will help them achieve development. But, many times, these individuals have positions that allow for no variety and/or little to no growth or professional development. They also typically provide no hope of being promoted or gaining new skills. Think about the boss who never says thank you, I appreciate you or great work. This triggers stress. The limited room for growth and lack of positive feedback makes people feel stuck, sick, robotic, underappreciated and unfulfilled.

5. Work-Life Balance

The truth is, most ambitious professionals like me don't know what work-life balance is. It doesn't come naturally to us, so we have to schedule it to achieve it. People of color who are workaholics have a hard time with this concept, because in our communities we glorify the idea of #teamnosleep, #nodaysoff, and #grind24/7. Or we can't afford not to work. And if we do take time off, we are still consumed by strict deadlines, answering emails, and fretting over tasks we failed to complete before we went on vacation. This defeats the purpose of having time off. Balance is a quintessential part of effectiveness. So stop responding to those emails and phone calls and start focusing on self-care. Please and thank you!

Show of hands—how many of you have experienced work-related stress due to the factors listed above? If not you, how many of you know someone who has? Although I can't see your hands, I can still *feel* them. Some of you have both hands up right now—or should, anyway. How do I know this? Well, you are reading this book, after all. FYI: Work-related stress can kill you! Furthermore, it is bad for you, your team, your employer, and the business. But I don't need to tell you this, do I?

Stressed employees cannot be the best versions of themselves, and as a result, something is missed or ineffectively handled, and everyone suffers as a result. In fact, according to a 2014 work stress survey, 80% of employees are stressed at work and 42% of employees admit having left a job due to stress (The American Institute of Stress, 2019). It's 2019, so can you imagine how much these statistics have increased since 2014. Oh, and let's not forget about fussy stress-inducing clients and self-inflicted stress. Developing clear boundaries can help you remain stress-free.

Now, imagine the stress situations listed above, but with the added stress of juggling a toxic work environ-ment, pay gap, discrimination, and bias. Whoa! Seriously, how much more can women of color take? Working at any job can be stressful; however, being a woman of color while also keeping your blood pressure down, skin glowing, glutes toned, hair conditioned (shiny and healthy), spirits high, and remaining positive at work and home—is a lot.

No, the answer is not a bottle of red wine every night...although that doesn't sound bad (wink). I can't say I have all the answers—my main goal is to share what I wish I knew earlier during my time working in corporate America. The good news is that there are ways you can better manage work-related stress.

Now, let's talk about general stress, life stress, relationship stress, family stress, kids stress, and situational stress. Honestly, we could all use a little woosah from time-to-time. Period.

But what if...

You were up late at night tossing and turning because of a to-do list and the accompanying thoughts that are holding your brain hostage and preventing you from resting properly. Your mind wanders right before bedtime every night, determined to prevent you from sleeping soundly. This sleeplessness occurs a few times a week.

You finally manage to doze off two or three hours before it's time to get up **(Stress Level 2).** Because you didn't get enough sleep, you wake up with a massive headache, so you hit snooze on your clock several times. When you finally get up you are 15 minutes behind schedule. You crawl out of bed and stub your pinky toe on the bottom railing that your husband *still* hasn't fixed—even after the thirtieth request. You become angry at your husband because he hasn't done what you asked him to do **(Stress Level 3).** The pain in your pinky toe is so bad, you wonder if it's broken. And now the throbbing in your head and toe are in sync.

"Get up, Ladybug!" you yell to your daughter, who is determined to milk *your* tardiness with a few extra minutes of sleep. Finally, you are both dressed and ready to go. Then she reminds you that she needs purple glue sticks for a project that is due today! **(Stress Level 4).** Agitated, you reach for your phone to check the time. You notice that you have two urgent email notifications from your boss. While motioning for "Ladybug" to get in the car, you skim the content of the email. That is when it hits you—you drafted a response to the original email yesterday but forgot to hit Send. Yikes! As a result, an executive's flight didn't get changed from a 2PM to a 4PM arrival. Your heartbeat accelerates, and now you are frustrated and super stressed **(Stress Level 6)**. You drive to Walgreens in a hurry and feverishly run from aisle to aisle looking for colored glue sticks, all the while quietly praying that you can get the executive on the later flight. Also, on your mind is your husband's inconvenient work schedule and how he's no help with your daughter in the mornings.

You find the purple glue sticks on aisle 12. You purchase them, jump in your car and fly out of the parking lot like you're practicing for the Indy 500. You zoom down the street, so you can get your daughter to school in time for breakfast...but then you hear a siren behind you. Guess what? You're now at a **Stress Level 10**. The siren is in your rearview window. It's blaring for *you*.

You pull over and a cop walks up and gives you a ticket for going over the speed limit in a school zone. You were maybe going five miles over the speed limit, but because your daughter is in the car, you doubt you went over much more than that. You explain that to him, but he is unwavering.

You take the ticket and go on your merry way. The delay has made your daughter miss the school breakfast, so now you first have to get your daughter's food from a drive-through. Your daughter's late, and you're almost a half hour late to work yourself. And to make matters worse, you still haven't changed the executive's flight. On a scale of 1-10, you are now at a Stress Level 15, and you haven't even set foot in your office. How do you think the workday will go?

These life and circumstantial examples are real. In fact, each sequence of events produces additional stress. So, imagine what happens when we experience stress at all ends, i.e., at home, in life, *and* at work. Well, the answer is there is little to no reprieve, and our health suffers. Now that you understand that stress is unavoidable, the best way to get ahead of it is to reduce it as much as you can.

If you are less stressed at work, there will be a lower chance of the stress following you home. And if you have less stress at home, you'll have a better chance of not being stressed at work. So what can you do? Change courses when you feel your stress levels rising. Have a strategy in place, and refrain from transferring your stress onto others. Help is on the way!

Rahkal's Simple Woosah Guide to Managing Life and Work Stress

I. Get Organized & Prioritize

Get organized. Prioritize your time with a to-do list. Leave a little flex room in case something urgent comes up and you're thrown off course. This is especially true if you have little ones, because nothing ever goes to plan. However, with proper planning things will run more smoothly. So, Sis, don't pack your schedule, leave some room in your day for the unexpected. If nothing comes up, you can use that extra time to focus on yourself. But, don't share this extra time! It's yours, so take a break!

2. Speak Up & Say NO!

Advocating for yourself and other WOC is one of the best things you can do to build confidence and reduce stress. Speaking up holds individuals accountable and helps reduce workplace injustices (even if you don't see a change immediately). Ever heard the phrase better out than in? Speak up even if you think you're being mishandled. Have a conversation. Acknowledge your grievances and stressors, write them down, and assess them closely. Initiate conversations about what you need to feel safe and productive in the workplace. Your voice is powerful and necessary! Also say *no* and mean it. If it is completely out of your job description or it will conflict with something of a higher priority and significance, say *no*. If it will lead to a hefty dose of stress, say *no*. Or, if you prefer something less harsh, use words like, "Unfortunately," "I can't…" or "I'm so sorry—I wish I could, but I don't have the time to do that right now." Remember every time you say yes to someone or something else you're saying no to you.

3. Let It Ring!

Do not answer! Send the person to voicemail. You don't have to always respond to calls, texts, or notifications. I get that we are a "microwave culture" that says we must answer *every* call, text, and message, but that simply isn't true. Today, people want 24/7 access to everything, and they want it *now*.

On the other hand, please don't feel like you need to be responsive and accessible every minute of every day, because you don't. In fact, when you feel like you must respond no matter what, it undermines your boundaries and heightens your stress level, especially when you're repeatedly answering draining calls and texts from people (including family members) you don't have the energy for. Who are your "faucets"? Who are your "drains"? Are you being drained? If so, just say *no!*

4. Table It

Can it wait until tomorrow, or is it important or urgent? You know there is a difference between these two situations. *Important* means the task must be completed.

Urgent means the task requires an immediate response. If it doesn't require this type of response and it's time for you to work on something else, table it until the next day. So prioritize your day accordingly. And remember: Just because it's important doesn't mean it's urgent.

5. Last Call

Manage your time wisely and set a cut-off time. Then, stick to it. For example, you could say something like this: "Today, I am going to aim to complete five tasks (from most important to the least)—and that will be it. My cut-off time today will be 4:30PM, and I will *not* start anything new after that time. I will not be guilted into helping with or taking over someone else's responsibilities. My goal is to focus on perfecting my own abilities and tasks." This can also apply to both personal and work tasks. So take that last call—and then cut it off. Designate times for specific things. Is Sunday your follow-up day or relaxation day? If you routinely use this day to follow up or relax, keep that boundary.

Speaking of boundaries…

6. Boundaries

Read Chapter 6.

7. Minimize Personal Stress

Get a good night's sleep, and don't sweat the small stuff or anything that is out of your control. Stop majoring on the minor! Also, don't over-commit, and focus on maintaining your health.

8. Mindset Shift

Shift your thought processes to reduce stress. Change your perspective on how you view things, including yourself, and the tasks you will accomplish that day.

9. Delegate

Assign tasks to other team members whenever possible. This can help reduce the number of things you will need to do that day. Do not be too proud to ask for help.

10. Reward

Treat yourself; celebrate any small victories. Also, reward yourself for the things you are doing right. Be good to yourself. It's easy to point out where we've slacked or the things we've done wrong. So, do something different and focus on what you *have* successfully accomplished. You work hard, so be sure to play hard. Hello!

CHAPTER SIX

BOUNDARIES!

Allow Me to Reintroduce Myself

Have you ever been in a situation where a boss asked you to stay late, come early, or work unscheduled times? What about the coworker, classmate, or associate approached you and said or did something you just didn't like? When this happened, did you make your displeasure known, shake it off, or chalk it up to a one-time incident? Let me guess—you didn't want to make a scene, or you wanted to be a team player, so you let it ride. I get it—the offending person seemed so kind, accommodating, and friendly that you didn't want to come across as being uptight. So, you simply went with the flow.

You probably told yourself, *I'm sure it was unintentional, or they really need my help. They didn't mean any harm by what they said or did. I may be overthinking it or being too sensitive. I don't want to seem unapproachable. Am I* right? Well, guess what? I've been there, too. I can tell you, that approach would be okay *if* you didn't have to see or work with that person again. But for most of us, that's just not realistic. And because you must see or report to this person every day at work, that behavior was and still is unacceptable. As a matter of fact, the behavior lingers. Now what? That same thing you didn't want to make a big deal out of continues to resurface every time you encounter the person. Depressing, right? My goal is to be honest with you, no matter what. That example is why it is so important that you set *boundaries* as early as possible in your employment. Boundaries are crucial in the workplace.

They are especially vital when establishing relationships with colleagues. I genuinely believe that we train people how to treat us. We have the power to accept or decline what's handed to us. If something doesn't feel right or isn't good for your energy, morals, or spirit— don't accept it. You don't have to. Got it?

In this chapter I'll share a few stories and scenarios— all real occurrences and prime examples of the need for boundaries. These stories eloquently illustrate how the lack of boundaries can cause distress. We'll conclude the chapter with a few points of discussion and an activity.

Let's explore exactly what boundary means:

bound a ry
/ˈbound(ə)rē/

A line that marks the limits of an area; a dividing line.

Most of us know what boundaries are and why we need them. But why is it so hard to set them? Why do we intentionally engage in conversations and permit unacceptable and uncomfortable behaviors from others? I'll keep it simple for those struggling to identify needed boundary areas. Think about what causes discomfort, annoyance, emotional drain, or pain in the workplace. These are the areas where you need to set boundaries.

Listen, if you engage in or allow something unpleasant to happen once or twice, you have subconsciously opened the door to allow continued access to off-limit topics and behavior.

Most trespassers are oblivious and "just being themselves." However, some people are intentional button-pushers and manipulative. Maybe you let them into your life out of a desire to feel relatable, relevant, to fit in, or be approachable. Maybe you're reluctant to speak up because everyone accepts that individual's inappropriate behavior…so you do, too. Sometimes, we enjoy engaging in behavior that we know we shouldn't. Well, don't sweat it and don't be too hard on yourself. It's human nature. We've all been there. That's why I'm here—to give you a few practical tips on how to recognize when you need boundaries, how to set them up, and how to re-establish boundaries, even if you have allowed foolery in the past.

Okay, I have to talk about hair for just a few. Sounds simple, but it's certainly an area where boundaries are needed.

"Your hair is so neat."

"Your hair is so *fun*."

In your opinion, is calling someone's hair "neat" or "fun" an insult or a compliment? Well, one of the most amazing things about being a black woman is our limitless creativity when expressing ourselves through our natural crowns...our hair. We can press it, curl it, braid it, twist it, weave it, finger wave it, rock an Afro, spike it, fade it, or just let it be.

For centuries, the hair and features of women of color have been considered undesirable. Our features have been unpopular and described as "wild," "unruly," and/or unattractive by non-black individuals. Our physical attributes simply aren't celebrated in mainstream culture. European features have been the standard, the bar, and a model of what beauty *should* look like in America. Now, imagine not conforming to this standard at the workplace. Imagine how others may perceive your non-standard imagery as a threat.

For instance, a black teenager in New Jersey was given the choice of having to either cut his hair in the middle of a wrestling match or forfeit the match. Seriously! And this is only one of many stories. In fact, there are countless stories of people of color being sent home from work and school, not being hired or promoted, experiencing racial profiling, and other types of discriminations because of the way they have chosen to wear their hair.

The truth is that people of color are often told that their natural hair isn't professional, or that it's distracting. We get told this so much so that some states and companies have begun to crack down on hair discrimination. It's shameful that it was necessary for hair discrimination laws to be created and enforced. I'm only thirty-five, but I can still recall hearing about hair when I was a kid. It was a big thing for black women who were interviewing for jobs. Sadly, I grew up believing that straightening or slicking one's hair was more professional-looking than wearing it in its natural state.

Fast forward to 2023. White CEOs are tattooed and executives are pierced with multi-colored hair. One of my previous CEOs was. Although, I couldn't imagine him being black and able to garner that title, let alone be tatted and black. Times have definitely changed. And for black women, there has been an overwhelming emergence of pride when it comes to our hair. We are now proudly wearing our hair in its natural state—i.e., unrelaxed, unbothered, and unfiltered. Despite the ugly double standard and puzzling reactions by non-minorities, we are embracing the choice to wear our hair any way we please. However, changing our hair *still* is reason for some white people to make a big fuss. They always seem fascinated. It's almost like these individuals view us like circus animals that they can touch and pet. In my case, neglecting to set proper boundaries when it came to my hair ended in tragedy. I have had many things said about my hair, from observations that it looked "neat" to "Is it real?" "How does it smell?" "How do you wash it—or *do* you wash it?", etc. For years, for the sake of educating the clueless and satisfying their curiosity, the younger me never set boundaries for my hair.

Truth be told, I neglected to set boundaries at work then, period. Therefore, I was *stuck* being uncomfortable around many of my colleagues. But do you want to know what was worse? People feeling entitled. More specifically, people thinking they have a right to touch or "pet" my hair without my permission. I hate having my personal space invaded; that is soooo disrespectful.

Seriously, didn't your mother teach you not to touch people?

Of course, it would be wrong for me to react with a quick uppercut, as appealing as that option might be. We are tired of holding press conferences about our hair at work. It's annoying, frustrating, and stressful to have to plot how to redirect people from talking about you or touching you. FYI: Some hair comments and inquiries are not innocent, but intentional. In those cases, shut it down immediately. You don't have to even respond…at least not with words. So, instead of adopting the circus approach, people should follow a museum approach…look, but don't touch! Better yet would be to not even look…just let us be. I don't know any woman of color who treats non-minorities in the insensitive manner black women are treated at work, especially when it comes to our hair.

I'll say this: Anything that triggers distress or prevents you from being productive at work *must* stop immediately, even if it's something as seemingly innocent as hair.

What about that creepy male colleague found in most offices; let's call him Bobby. Bobby likes giving hugs. He's boisterous, but not really funny. He is, however, seemingly popular, dresses nice, wears way too much cologne, and appears to be a smooth-talking ladies' man. After a few conversations, he starts to hug you. And I'm not talking about a "church hug." No, I'm talking about full-on chest-to-chest, pelvis-to-pelvis hugs. Those are what he gives. In all fairness, he hugs all the female colleagues and apparently wanted to include you in the rotation. The thing that puzzles you (aside from wondering why no one has reported his behavior to human resources) is that he doesn't seem to see anything wrong with his behavior. He is also often seen in colleagues' cubicles, chatting and sometimes sharing inappropriate stories about his weekend activities.

Did I fail to mention just how handsome and charming Bobby is? Because he is, and he knows it, using it as a pass to perpetuate his inappropriate behavior. He is also, despite his reputation as a ladies' man, *very married*. Your coworkers seem to like the attention he gives them, thus reinforcing his behavior. You, on the other hand, typically keep it short and sweet when talking to him.

But one day you entertained a conversation a little longer than usual, and afterward he began making it a point to visit your workstation—frequently. You didn't express any objections...and then the visits went from every other day to *every* day.

You become uncomfortable whenever you see him coming your way, and before you know it, he gets in that hug. He always seems to catch you off-guard. The first hug happened as you were walking to your desk. Bobby abruptly approached you and greeted you with a bear hug. It irritated you as well as made you uncomfortable, but you didn't know what to say. You really didn't want to make a big deal out it. You cringed at the thought of confronting him and asking him not to touch you and not even visit your desk anymore. You didn't say anything because, well, it's just a hug, and he hugs everyone, you try to reason with yourself. This is the behavior allowed in your office.

Then, there are the fake empathy and masked gossip folks at work. You learn the story of Diana. Diana's husband was diagnosed with brain cancer and has been out of work for two years with treatment. Their home is going into foreclosure, and she always comes to work looking tired and beat down. She's visibly depressed, wearing black all the time and could use some color in her wardrobe. "I just feel so bad for her," says one of her coworkers, whom we'll call "Sarah."

Sarah is similar to the personality type discussed earlier in the toxic environment example. She's is a mess starter. She's the type who throws rocks and then hides her hands. She interlopes in people's personal lives by befriending them and pretending to care. She sends social media friend requests pretending like she wants to be friends. And during lunch, she dissects everyone's Facebook posts—e.g., what they're doing outside of work and what they wear while doing it. She is influential, manipulative, and very deceptive. She has mastered the art of infiltration and gossip warfare. This is the type of person you need to avoid and limit conversations to business matters. Keep in mind that you can't share anything with her that you're not comfortable sharing with others.

There is also "Negative Nancy," who is always complaining about how much she hates the boss, hates

BOUNDARIES!

the company, the team, and how nothing goes right. However, she has no intention of leaving or doing anything to change her circumstances. She simply gripes every chance she gets. She never has a great weekend and believes everyone is against her. Her energy is terribly toxic and difficult to withstand. Finally, there is Jeffery. He's notorious for using unnecessary slangs around you in hopes of sounding "black." He gloats about living in an urban neighborhood as if this solidifies his usages of slang (that you would never use). He is demeaning and often microaggressive in his actions and words.

So, you have several forces, factors, personalities, and situations that you're up against at work. Nevertheless, your mission is to get your job done, utilize your skills, gain new ones, keep your head low, and be out. With your mission in mind, you allow things to remain as they are… but it's impacting your ability to thrive in the workplace. The culture is like a vacuum—easy to get sucked in.

When we are silent, we unintentionally subscribe to things we otherwise would not. Silence speaks volumes. And boy, do we pay for it…eventually. All the examples and experiences described throughout this book are what kept me and the women I spoke with moving between the offices of HR, the liquor store and those of our respective doctors. Maybe you have experienced similar trauma, or this isn't your story. If it isn't, good for you! Hopefully, illustrating real-life experiences will provide you with a more in-depth insight on how to identify potential problems and prevent them from happening. Again, people will be people, and we can't control them, but you can control what you subject yourself to. If this is your story, it's not too late to re-establish yourself. You can set up boundaries at any time.

FYI: It's important to understand that if you decide to re-establish yourself and set boundaries later, there may be some consequences. For example, you may experience some emotional discomfort. But that's okay, because the reward will be more significant than any pain you may experience. *Peace is priceless.* You will hear me say this repeatedly. Say it with me: "Peace is priceless."

This peace will come after you rid yourself of excessive garbage. But be prepared to experience isolation while setting boundaries. Some people may be inclined to withdraw from you because of your new approach in setting boundaries.

You may also experience confusion on the part of your coworkers and accusations of "acting funny" or "thinking you're better than us." They may even accuse you of "changing." Well, don't feel bad about that...you *have* changed, but for the better. You now have boundaries in place when you didn't before. But you haven't changed who you are inside. You just put a stop to the things that don't serve you. So, if your coworkers feel you've changed—oh, well! We should all change, because this type of change equals growth.

This period of transition can be difficult, but it's for the best. Those who truly respect you will get over it. You have a right to change your mind at any time. You don't have to be who you were last year, last month, last week, or even three hours ago. You also don't have to accept what you did last year, last month, last week, or three hours ago. And you don't owe anyone anything. If something no longer suits you, pull the plug! Your colleagues will get over it, especially if they have to work with you day in and day out. After all, what are they going to do? Fire you for setting boundaries? I think not. You will still have to work together and remain professional.

Let's explore some boundary-based activities. Listed below are a couple of things you should keep in mind when setting or establishing limitations:

1. **Create a personal mission statement for your wellbeing (mental, physical, and emotional). Mission statements are great drivers for life. They keep you focused, on track and supportive of your WHY.**

   Here's one that I created just before my 35th birthday: *"Moving forward, I will protect my entire being, and anything that threatens to compromise my health, integrity, happiness, ability to grow, confidence, and peace must go. I will not compromise in those areas. I will always choose me."*

Now, jot down your statement. It can be simply a word or sentence, but you should put some thought into it. After you create it, memorize it and use it when making decisions.

_____

_____

_____

_____

_____
_____
_____

Great job (if you filled this in). After you have memorized it, keep it handy and use it as a guide for every uncomfortable situation, encounter, or obstacle you face. Put it on your desk and on your door at home as a reminder when you leave for the day. Make decisions with this mission statement in mind. If you find yourself doing something that contradicts your mission, *kill it, ASAP.*

2. Identify your deal breakers and areas of conflict.

I suggest you do this upfront *before* starting a new job, team, or even a relationship. If you're already in one of these and are looking to reintroduce yourself, this is still a great technique. Maybe your deal breakers are gossip, working off the clock, an invasion of personal space (physically and conversationally), poor communication, injustices or favoritism, being too friendly at work, and/or colleagues and social media.

What if you're on a team with a terrible communicator or a lazybones? How much are you willing to give and to allow? You will need to identify this and write it down. For those who have been on their job for a while, take a moment to write down your current challenges and the things that bother you. Think about what makes you cringe, clam up, or want to leave.

What are my deal breakers? What are my areas of conflict?

_____

_____

_____

_____

_____

_____

_____

_____

_____

_____

_____

So, decide if the situation or observation is compromising your integrity, mission statement, or what you believe in. If so, speak up and remove yourself from the situation. Be mindful to choose your battles wisely, but also stick firm to your boundaries.

3. Locate your boundary strategy

This looks different for everyone. Are you redirecting the incident/conversation, removing yourself from it, not answering after-hour communications, defending yourself, or speaking up? Think about the consequences of your actions when using this strategy. For instance, if you choose to do nothing, will it cost you too much? Keep in mind that having a strategy is critical so you don't get caught off guard, not knowing what to do when an incident occurs.

What is your new plan of action when encountering or experiencing overstepped boundaries?

_____
_____
_____
_____
_____
_____
_____
_____
_____
_____
_____
_____
_____

What is your talking point or the script that you'll say when a boundary is overstepped? Approaches will vary, but it's best to have something vs. nothing.

Example:

- *William, we're going to have to find a happy medium working together. Communication and punctuality are vital for us to work together successfully. (Will is often late and unresponsive to emails).*

- *Sarah, I really don't have the capacity to listen to anything negative today, or any day moving forward.*
- *Bobby, I'm going to have to ask you to stop approaching me for hugs. This makes me feel uncomfortable and invades my personal space.*
- *Jeffery, your comments are racially insensitive and offensive to me. Please use proper grammar when speaking to me as you would with senior leadership.*
- *Hey Nancy, I was thinking…shut the hell up for once!* (Okay, so I'm just kidding with that one.)

Your turn!

_____

_____

_____

_____

_____

_____

_____

_____

_____

_____

4. Social media "friend requests"

If you don't want to connect with colleagues, I suggest you search for and block your colleagues first, before they find you and request to be friends on social media. Some people use their photo with a nickname rather than their real name to prevent being befriended by professional contacts.

If they find you on social media before you've had a chance to block them, just ignore the request. If your colleagues mention that you haven't responded to their friend requests, politely say, "Hey, I prefer not be 'friends' with colleagues on social media, but I'm happy to connect with you on LinkedIn or any other professional network." Some of you are naturally unfiltered and will take a more direct approach by flat out saying, "Nope! Not today, Satan." LOL. Kudos to you.

What are some other social media strategies?

_____

_____

_____

_____

5. Create your own narrative

Narratives for people of color (specifically black and brown people) are often told for us by others. Many of these narratives and perspectives are unfounded and contradictory. In the workplace stereotypes such as incompetent and lazy exist. However, data supports black women as the most educated and ambitious among any other working groups. Outside of the workplace we're viewed as dangerous, violent, criminal and a threat to culture. The hypocrisy of this is that whites originated violence, hate, terror, murdering and criminal acts against blacks for centuries. Our country was built on murdering, assaulting and inflicting terror on people. Fast-forward to present day. While Klan's men are no longer publicly riding around on horses in hoods they are riding around in patrol cars with badges and in the courtrooms, class-rooms and certainly the workplace.

From the early 1900s to Jim Crow, blacks were treated and portrayed in demeaning and egregious manners. This same treatment was highly perpetuated in the media, in inaccurate narratives, in policy, systems and among other non-minorities. So here we are fighting an uphill battle to dismantle false narratives and corrupt systems. Therefore, the best way to set boundaries regarding narrative is to write your own and for our white allies, please speak up and out against gossip and potentially damning narratives you may hear about blacks. Antiracism must be priority.

I define gossip as a false narrative created about someone by someone else. We've talked plenty about gossip, and the basic message is, don't partake! Leave when others start to engage in it. If getting away isn't feasible, add a positive perspective to the conversation or topic. Redirect and deflect, and turn the salacious into something positive. Trust me, doing this will likely kill most of the drama in its tracks. Keep counteracting nega-tive rhetoric with positivity and optimism.

Yes, this takes energy but helps maintain your peace. Consider speaking with your supervisor or HR about ways to boost morale and about the challenges of working with the team or a specific person. Documentation comes in handy here. Listing credible incidents can help support your position with management. Just be sure to detail how these behaviors impede your ability to be productive.

Another way to get ahead of false narratives is by volunteering limited information...*but*, only share what you're comfortable being repeated. It's important to build genuine relationships in the workplace. This can be done via vulnerability. If you do this, you (not others) will drive your narrative. I know that sharing information is difficult for us, reason being, a large majority of black people (at least the ones I know) abide by a different code of ethics. I like to call it the "we mind our own business" code. For example, we don't disclose our personal business as freely as some other folks, nor are we interested in asking about other people's business. Furthermore, many black households had these popular sayings: "What goes on in this house, *stays* in this house!" "Why you dippin' in the Kool-Aid and don't know the flavor?" and "I ain't got nothin' to do with that!"

In essence, each saying equates to minding your own business!

Our code of ethics helps us to stay out of the workplace drama. For the most part, we like to keep it moving. I will admit that sometimes minding our own business can get sticky when others voluntarily share their personal business, and I mean *all* of their personal business. It gets sticky because the person sharing their business maybe under the false impression that you'll do the same. Some even have a sense of entitlement (the Karen persona), believing they have a right to know what's happening in your life, as well. Well, they don't. You're not obligated to anyone or anything. However, if you choose to circumvent speculation by sharing things, keep it minimal. Learn to master the art of sharing very little information in a way that makes others feel like they know more about you than they really do. Keep in mind that not knowing facts doesn't stop people from making things up and *presenting* it as fact.

Don't rule out the intimidation factor. Because you're a brilliant woman of color, people are intimidated by you! I've learned that people fear what they do not understand, know, or can't conquer. Therefore, creating a false narrative about someone or something makes sense—if you are intimidated by it. Why? Well, because it comforts the storyteller, gossiper, or negative person. In other words, it makes them feel that they (not you) are in control of what they know or think of you. Even if done in a joking or subtle manner, do not allow anyone to create a false narrative or half-truth about you. I repeat, do *not* let this happen. When you allow people to create these types of narratives for or about you, you give them creative power over your story (truth).

White Savior Syndrome

A prime example: A former coworker who was determined to "figure me out" would frequently make suggestive comments about me to others. She would say things like, "Rahkal has all the guys stopping by to see her," "Rahkal must take hours to get ready in the morning," "Rahkal sure gets a lot of attention. I bet she loves this," etc. Her suggestions would be insignificant, but were also baseless and untrue. Again, these were subtle ways to learn more about me. Because the comments didn't mean much to me, I let them slide. However, I should have set a boundary by correcting her. She eventually started calling me, "Sister," but I refused to get cozy with her. I intentionally sidestepped personal questions and started to keep my reports of weekend activities and solicited opinions very vague.

We started off on the wrong foot after my hiring. Interestingly, she jokingly admitted to having been intimidated by me during my interview process (which the supervisor allowed her to sit in on). That was an obvious sign to me to stay clear. Cunning and manipulative, she played the game very well. She was a master at it, actually. Consequently, I had neglected to set firm boundaries with her from the very beginning. My strategy at the time was to lay low. For instance, I didn't speak up or correct her when she made inappropriate remarks about me here and there. Why not? Because I honestly didn't want to deal with confrontation; nor did I see what was happening at first. Eventually, I picked up on her modus operandi. Once she learned that I was onto her, we became frenemies. Determined to *conquer* me, her false narratives kicked up in a higher gear. She started to paint me as a helpless and needy "poor soul." And in case you're wondering, yes, she was a white woman.

I didn't want to deal with her, so I laughed or shrugged things off or simply excused myself. Please, don't do this. Yes, some battles should be carefully chosen, but use discretion. I should have picked this battle, because as time went on, her painting me as helpless began to be infuriating and humiliating.

As the only black woman in our area, I couldn't help but think of the white savior syndrome. This syndrome refers to white people who pretend to help and support non-whites, but this help and support is purely self-serving. Think of movies like *Hidden Figures, Get Out,* and *The Blind Side.*

One day she decided to talk about my finances to a group of people in an effort to "help" me. "I know what it's like not to have two nickels to rub together, and still need to pay bills and feed a family," she said. Granted, my colleagues were aware that I was caring for two children in my family at the time. However, I have never and would never discuss my personal finances with colleagues, but this was her perspective and the narrative she created for me. Flabbergasted, I didn't know what to say. I was the only brown face in a conversation about my finances that I did not initiate! Raging inside, I kept cautioning myself, *be mindful not to appear like the angry Black woman.* Part of me couldn't believe she had said that, and while I wanted to give them all a piece of my mind, I said nothing. I didn't know how to defend myself in that moment or environment.

Unfortunately, my silence co-signed the false narrative that she had created about me. As a result, there were times when I would return to my desk after a lunch or restroom break and find loaves of bread sitting on my desk. Someone had left it for me to presumably take home to my family. Colleagues and even senior executives brought in a hand-me-down coat to give me, as well. One person actually gave me some pants…I'm not kidding. Leftovers from catered lunch meetings were often packaged up for me. It became an embarrassing nightmare.

While I'm sure my coworkers (some of them) were trying to be kind, these gestures made me feel inferior, especially as the only black woman with white support staff and executives. Are you horrified reading this, too? It's embarrassing for me to even share it. Uncomfortable and voicing a mumbled thanks, I took the garments only to discard them. Although I must admit that I did eat the food that I liked. One last thing and I'll put the story to rest. The finale of this coworker's "kindness" came just in time for the holidays. She initiated taking up a collection for me and my "needy" family for Christmas. She asked senior level executives, our boss, and other colleagues in the department to chip in to help me financially. She positioned it as if they had collectively chosen my family to sponsor for the holidays. After the fact I learned that this wasn't something the company did. They never sponsored a particular employee's family for the holidays. I was a first.

While the gesture appeared to be kind (on the surface), it was still humiliating and coming from a self-serving space. Her charitable act was more for her benefit than mine. She likely positioned herself as caring and benevolent. As for the money, I bought toys for the children and we used the rest feeding the homeless. That said, the funds were well spent. She never once considered how any of this would make me feel or how I would be perceived by everyone else. It all possibly could have been avoided had I spoken up and put boundaries in place from our first encounter. She wasn't the first White Savior personality that I've encountered either. A white male ED of a nonprofit that I worked for had a track record of white saviorism to boost his image. He often positioned himself as an ally to the underprivileged black and brown youth we "served" but failed to truly build with or get to know them personally. In many cases he exploited them for funding and notoriety positioning.

It's important to evaluate and assess motives with individuals. If you pay close attention you're more likely to identify where the origins of someone's intentions. When something doesn't sit right with you, you've got to speak up, inquire and challenge authenticity even if it doesn't impact you. Remember, silence is a stance.

6. Friends at work

Be cautious, vigilant, and deliberate from Day One. Remember, everyone isn't able to separate the personal from the professional. This is not to say you can't make friends at work, because you most likely will. But, try to stick with mature and authentic people. Make observations to assess authenticity. Pay attention to see if personal conversations surface at the job. This could be a red flag. Also, consider avoiding after-hour meetups unless you really trust the person. However, I recommend keeping a professional divide. This boundary helps to reduce scrutiny associated with familiarity. My grandma would say it like this, "Don't be getting too familiar with those people."

Ever heard the phrase "familiarity breeds contempt?" I've found this to be true. When people think they know you, they tend to underestimate and lose respect for you. A loss of respect can negatively impact your position in the workplace. So, form healthy relationships organically and with people who are positive and uplifting—not the gloomy ones who drag others down with them. You will know the difference. The best thing about this type of friendship is that it's natural and nurturing. The right friendships are vital, especially at work. We all need allies to survive in challenging environments. But it is also important to set boundaries, even with your friends in the workplace. We will talk about building a trusted tribe and community in the next chapter. But for now, be selective as to who you consider a friend, and also be cautious about how much personal information you share with them. You are not obligated to connect with colleagues after work or even at lunch, and you don't owe explanations, either. Be selective. I have witnessed situations where one colleague thought other colleagues were her friends, only to end up exposed with a knife in her back.

Another challenge with work friends is that if a disagreement or falling out occurs and that friendship goes south, unnecessary tension is added to the work environment, making it difficult to be professional on the job. If possible, avoid allowing work friends to believe you are closer than you really are. Setting this boundary helps to prevent backlash and a world of confusion. Trust me, I have been here, and I know it's harder to pull back after the fact.

The goal of this lesson is to make clear how important it is to set clear expectations and boundaries. The friendships that you'll make on the job will come naturally and authentically. My final advice on boundary setting is to *never* allow others make you feel guilty for protecting your peace. *Remember, you don't owe anyone a damn thing!* Stay true to who you are and who you see in the mirror every day. If you aren't feeling something or someone…make it known! Give yourself permission to speak up, leave, tune out, or shut it down. Keep your work and personal lives separate, within reason. You are there to do a job—not to please people. Establishing boundaries *early,* at the beginning of a job, conversation, relationship, or partnership, is imperative for success. Make sure others understand what you will or will not allow or tolerate. Thinking ahead and being direct is a huge timesaver, and a great way to be prepared for anything. You've got this!

CHAPTER SEVEN

COMMUNITIES AND TRIBES

Build Them

S is, there are no islands, and everyone got to where they are in their careers, at work, and in life with S-U-P-P-O-R-T! Don't let anyone tell you differently. The notion of "I don't need anyone" is immature and ridiculous. We all need someone, and we are all connected to people in one way or another. That said, I do not believe in the phrase "self-made." Granted, many of us have done the heavy lifting at times with little to no support, and many of us feel we are the ones making things happen. I get it. That is my story. In fact, I consider myself an independent woman who picked herself up with a will to thrive. My unique story is one of resilience. I'm sure yours is, too. It's our stories that provide exceptional perspective, equipping us with diverse strategies and contributions for the work-place. I said it before and I'll say it again: Our essence (and embracing it) is the key to thriving in corporate. Here's a little of my backstory:

I was born on the South Side of Chicago to a 19-year-old heroin and cocaine addict who dropped out of ninth grade. My mom first became pregnant with my older brother at age 14 and then had me. I grew up around drugs, domestic violence and in poverty. My father cut out when I was 5 years old. I attended low-performing schools and didn't have a 529 college savings plan, and I certainly didn't have family who left me a home in their will (Will? What's that?). I had no head start in life. I didn't have any role models or mentors. Perhaps you didn't, either. Maybe your story isn't as crazy as mine, or maybe it's worse. Whatever your story is, it doesn't have to end the same way it began, and there is power in it.

By the grace of God, I was the first in my family to graduate high school, the first to graduate from college and the first to earn a Master's degree. I beat all the statistics, naysayers, and projections of where I should have ended up. I worked my way into some of the biggest companies in the country. If anyone knows anything about feeling "self-made," it would be me—not that I consider myself self-made (because I don't); I just totally get it. I also don't believe in coincidences. I genuinely believe there is a force greater than all of us, orchestrating the strings, contacts, encounters, opportunities, and connec-tions in our lives. But, hey, that's just me. I'm not trying to force my beliefs on you.

What I am here to tell you in here in Chapter Seven is that behind every successful woman of color is a story filled with a tribe of others supporting, rooting for, and cheering her on. Maybe these tribes were invisible and not in the forefront, but they were present at critical times and places in your journey. Maybe it was that stranger who paid you a compliment on a difficult day, or that college counselor who helped you straighten out your financial aid situation. Maybe it was that teacher who believed in you, the other woman of color, on the interview panel, who advocated for you behind closed doors and helped you get the job. Whoever these Godsends were, they were there to help you along the way.

Tribes are critical to maintaining your sanity, peace, and success. Your tribe/community may come in various ways, colors, people, and times in your career. Many of your communal relationships may have been organically built, but it is in your best interest to also build with intentionality. As with any relationship, you will need to first "court" the person and nurture the relationship, so that it grows. Networking works the same way. Through networks and networking, you can build a community this way. First, let me define what networking is *not*. Networking is *not* what others can do for you. It is *not* a "what you can get" mentality.

Networking is, on the other hand, offering assistance, cultivating relationships ("Hey, happy Friday, just checking on you, I didn't want anything"), supporting people's businesses, purchasing their products, showing up at their events, etc. It is also being visible and having something worthwhile to offer, as well. Therefore, networking is a mutually beneficial relationship. It should focus on what you can offer and what support you can provide.

This makes transitions easier when opportunities become available or when you need someone to talk to. No, I am not suggesting that you be the only one doing the giving; rather, switch your mind to giving vs. receiving. The more you give and serve, the more you will get back in return. Doing this lays a strong foundation and provides a more natural way of connecting with individuals to build your community.

Joining business resource/affinity groups at your company and remaining very active helps. I joined Toastmasters, affinity groups, volunteered, got a gym membership onsite, and was very intentional and visible.

As a result, my community grew. It was comprised of diverse people, including senior leaders, mail clerks, food service workers, security personnel, and even janitors. Neither my title nor the department I worked in made me believe I was beyond building a community with different people within the company. Although most of my community consisted of people of color, I was still intentional about connecting with people of all races, ethnicities, and genders.

However, being a minority in a white-dominated environment who experienced frequent microaggressions sometimes made it feel difficult to connect with nonminorities. Filtering through who were genuine and who weren't was exhausting. Outside of work, I have friends from all races, creeds, and walks of life, so generally, diversity isn't a problem. But as a minority working in a corporate environment, connecting with other people of color provided a stronger sense of safety, trust, community, and family.

It may not be the same for you, and that's fine. The main point is for you to locate and build a community, so you're safe to speak freely, with no filters or mask. But do make sure your community consists of people who are empathetic, genuine, and open to you, as well—people who offer positive and constructive feedback, and who can be a non-judgmental ally for you.

Speaking of allies, I'm usually faced with how whites can better support women of color in the workplace. My advice is to assess your own potential implicit biases. Do some introspective work. Do you wrestle with superiority complexes or faulty perceptions about women of color? Have you bought into stereotypes? If so, humble and educate yourself. Learn from and have intentional conversations with black and brown women. You can also show more compassion and empathy. Just because something isn't your experience doesn't mean it isn't ours. And many things that are not your experiences are nightmares for us. Listen to learn, be accountable, and support us by being equity advocates and antiracists.

Granted, it's not your responsibility to pay for the sins of all racist white people. We don't expect you to, but we want you to check others you know engaging in discriminatory, biased, and racist behaviors and conversations when you hear them. Advocate for those you know or suspect may be mistreated. Do everything you can to ensure the environments you're in are equitable and inclusive.

It is also essential for women of color to have a personal advocate in the workplace. Ideally, this person is more seasoned and influential, and can provide coaching and support for your workplace needs. An advocate can help with promotions, exposure and opportunities.

The friendships, relationships, and camaraderie you build while working provides a sense of belonging. Seeing my friends and community was a big incentive for me. In fact, the twelve other professional women I spoke with felt the same. Although I didn't know each woman personally, it felt like we were all fighting a very similar battle and bogged down with similar issues. Across the board, we all felt isolated, unheard, unappreciated, unequally compensated, undervalued, and mistrusted.

One of the women, a Southwest flight attendant, described several horror stories in which she experienced blatant and inflammatory treatment and multiple incidents of racially charged verbal attacks and slurs by her colleagues, including pilots, flight crews, and even passengers. I was horrified, but not surprised. Typically the only woman of color on most flights or shifts, she had to pack extra patience and plaster on a disarming smile before being questioned, even badgered, about her hair, complexion, the books she has read, her facial features, body type, and a variety of other obscenities.

She's been poked, pushed, and called out of her name by white passengers. Recalling these tales was difficult for the flight attendant because there were times when she was called a nigger—even while checking into her hotel. She identified the states of Texas, Idaho, California, and Florida as being the most difficult to work in. In fact, one of her most challenging stories was that of her white colleague, a 27-year veteran flight attendant, who joked that she, the crew, and the captains wouldn't *lynch* her for providing an incorrect travel time. She filed a complaint but Southwest never responded with a follow-up or resolution.

I have also come across countless other disturbing stories, but fortunately, these women had *communities*... communities that were therapeutic for them. The flight attendant shared how it was her community explicitly that kept her from going rogue.

Speaking of therapeutic, my community didn't consist solely of other employees; my friends and closest relatives were also a part of it. Being able to connect with a diversely skilled community is healthy.

Your hairstylist, therapist, or even doctor can also be a part of your tribe. Both my hairstylist and doctor were part of mine, especially my doctor, who has been my primary advocate. My doctor was the one who recognized changes in my health and diagnosed work stress ailments. So ladies, make sure your community has variety, so you can receive all-inclusive perspectives and insights from different walks of life and different areas of life.

Your community will understand you. They'll provide you with a safe space to air out grievances while being vulnerable. With them, there is no need to wear a mask, dumb down your intellect, alter your tone, or be indirect when communicating. With my tribe, I certainly don't have to use inflection to avoid being viewed as aggressive or angry. Rather, I can share my unfiltered perspective and thoughts with them.

When I worked in corporate, for at least 30 minutes or an hour of my workday, I could be my true self and make jokes and references my companions understood. I didn't feel isolated, and I could freely refer to music and shows I'd heard or seen because I knew they'd probably heard or seen them, too. We often encouraged each other, chatted, laughed, and backed each other up. Interestingly, I must say that there is something about the glue that holds me and the women of color in my community together. It was not only work issues and similarities, but a more profound commonality.

Many of us were raised to be strong, unbreakable, and unemotional. Consequently, we ignored our feelings because "black women can take and handle anything." We were subconsciously fed this unhealthy mindset, which spilled over into our everyday practices, thus preventing us from speaking up and being seen or heard. Much of the drama that we endured or let slide in the work-place was because of this notion of strength, which inadvertently suggests that we don't *deserve* to be treated equally, don't *deserve* to be visible enough to be heard, because we can handle what we're given and make something out of nothing.

It's easier to silently allow things to happen in order to avoid confrontation. It is also easier to adopt a passive mentality that "We can take it" or "We can handle anything." Women of color, this ideology of unyielding strength is toxic and must stop! We *must* reach a space where we can be real, vulnerable, assertive, and transparent in the workplace—not only with the people in our communities, but with everyone we encounter. We *must* be realistic about our capacities and listen to and embrace our bodies and emotions.

We can do this by speaking up and letting our voices, ideas, and perspectives be known, seen, and heard. If something doesn't sit right with you, call it out unapologetically, and ask questions. Hold people, yourself, and your community accountable. You deserve equal treatment. You deserve to be stress-free and more. Don't wait until you're burned out, clocked out, or nearly explosive and atomic to make a change. That was me, and it wasn't pretty. Do *not* do this. Just before I resigned from my last corporate role, my colleagues saw an entirely different me. What they didn't realize was that my mask had swollen. It had become too heavy and was susceptible to erupting at any moment.

In my first 90 days on my former job, I clocked out (mentally). I was over it. Starting off on the wrong foot didn't help, and they definitely started me off on the wrong foot, as I was given the work of four people and stretched completely thin in multiple areas (aka, the corporate beatdown). Seriously, in less than three months I was doing multiple jobs. The bottom line was most important, superseding the methods used to achieve the end result. Working people equals bottom line accomplishments! Many companies are so fixated on goals that they forget their employees are their most valuable asset. Happy, healthy, and motivated employees reach the bottom line every time. And the real magic happens when leadership and employers realize their sole focus must shift from bottom lines and results to servicing, empowering, and amplifying their employees' strengths and needs. Bottom lines and results are not achieved by machines but through humans.

So not only was I overworked in my first few months, the discomfort associated with being an "only" factored in the equation. I experienced some form of micro-aggression roughly every other day. I didn't know how to defend myself without offending someone else. I didn't want to be stereotyped or to gain a target on my back because of an emotional response. All eyes were already on me—what I wore, how I styled my hair, my demeanor, and my overall presentation. The culture was cliquish, biased, messy, and toxic in many ways. In addition, my supervisor (a middle-aged white woman) was terribly ineffective, unprofessional, and insensitive.

The more she piled onto my plate, the more I ate. Not only was I new in the role, but it had also been a career shift. Therefore, it was a bit of a learning curve as well. It was the opposite of the type of work I was accustomed to doing. Because I didn't want to make a bad impression, I didn't voice any objections, choosing to champion through it instead. At that time I needed my job to support my family. However, all that "pushing through" came at the expense of my physical, mental, and emotional health.

Luckily, I had built a robust work community, and honestly, I needed them. They were a tremendous support system for me during that time. But by my first anniversary on the job, I had seen, been exposed to, and experienced it all. I didn't feel safe and was undoubtedly a ticking time bomb. Some people were friendly, and some experiences were fine; it wasn't *all* unpleasant. However, it all piled up badly for me, and much of it left me to shrink internally. Suppressing my voice, neglecting to set clear boundaries, mismanaging stress—everything that I am encouraging you to avoid. All these things came to bite me…and they bit hard.

If regular life stress had been reduced, then my work stress probably would have been more tolerable. If work stress had been reduced, then it wouldn't have amplified life stress. Life and work truly go hand in hand. We talked about woosah-ing and stress management in both areas in the previous chapter. Now you see why balancing the two is critical. Woosah, girl. WOOOOOSAH!

I finally decided to do something about it and to speak up, but by that time I was nearly debilitated. I had severe anxiety, sleep deprivation, and panic attacks; my blood pressure was astronomical. I had begun to have heart palpitations merely upon entering the building. At one point, I was convinced I was going to die at thirty-three—just like Jesus.

My doctor (also a community member) saved my life by ordering immediate time off, and I am so glad she did. I took a brief medical leave, and it was such a rejuvenating time for me. I meditated, painted, created, took yoga classes, read, rested, volunteered, and focused on regaining good health. Unfortunately, the stress triggered a few other health issues, but I didn't die! The time off provided an opportunity for me to recharge physically and also time to reevaluate my work life.

During this time, I decided I'd had enough, so I began to plan my corporate exit. It didn't happen overnight; rather, it was strategic. But, before I departed, I was committed to leaving the environment better than I found it. More specifically, I didn't just exit, but vowed to use my voice to support those who would come after me or who were in similar environments. I exited a previous position due to very similar toxicity. However, in that environment, not only was the director dishonest and microaggressive, but he also had a habit of reprimanding me in front of clients and staff. Much younger at the time, I opted to resign vs. fight. I didn't want to repeat the same mistake this time.

Like that role, my supervisor's (also the department's director) leadership style fostered the majority of the toxicity. Therefore, I had to reach out to someone higher in our org chart. This is why I mentioned the importance in knowing who reports to whom. Eventually, I filed a grievance citing all the inappropriate, discriminatory hostilities, immoral conduct, and mismanagement by leadership demanding an investigation and reconciliation.

Although I decided to leave months prior I knew I needed to speak up before leaving. My motive was to aid in making that space better than I found it. It was certainly risky and uncomfortable to speak out against systems and inappropriate behaviors while still working daily. However, had I just quit or filed a grievance and then quit there would have been little to no accountability.

Perhaps your experience won't come to this. Maybe it's very different. Either way, I hope you'll digest some of what I have shared and apply it for a better outcome. I'm rooting for you, Sis!

The last thing I want to leave you with is a couple of community building strategies. How about we go from surviving to thriving?

Activity time: Let's create an action plan for finding and building a tribe.

Do the following:

1. **List a couple of qualities that you'd like to see in the people you would like to surround yourself with.**

_____

_____

_____

_____

_____

_____

_____

_____(are you demonstrating these same qualities?)

2. Identify 2-3 people who you admire (from your company or specific department, alumni association, affinity group, class, church, or wherever), ask them out for coffee or tea and learn their stories. (*Be sure to inquire about their techniques on obtaining success and overcoming obstacles.*)

3. Keep in touch with the people in the previous example. Create calendar reminders to check in with them. Invite them places, ask to support them. Nurture these growing relationships!

4. Ensure your LinkedIn profile is updated, appropriate, and adequately depicts your skills. Connect with people there.

5. Identify 1-2 networking events or professional development opportunities, reach out to the organizer and ask how you can support them.

6. Join your alumni association, an affinity group, FB group, class, and go volunteer!

7. Practice being, doing, and giving what you would like to receive from your community.

CHAPTER EIGHT

WOOSAH

Survive to Thrive

We briefly talked about the need to woosah outside of work, right? It's important to have a healthy balance between your work and life. While some companies don't believe in, foster, or encourage a work-life balance, it's still essential. The responsibilities associated with your job can run you ragged if you let them. There are goals and deadlines to reach, but truthfully, when you are not healthy or sharp, everyone and everything else gets your scraps. And when you do not feel valued or respected, you cannot be your best self. It's impossible.

Sis, I know you want to do more than survive. I want you to, as well. As a matter of fact, it is my hope that you eventually thrive in corporate (if this is where you want to be). Scratch that; I would love to see you succeed in corporate, nonprofit, public sectors, business, entrepreneurship, relationships, and in all areas of your career and life.

That said, let's recap what we've learned and apply the basic principles below. Think of the lessons from stories shared. Here is an excellent way to jumpstart your thriving life, period. Just think about it.

1. Understand the **playing field**. This is about understanding where you are, what you're up against and your why. The playing field is applicable to all aspects of life. After understanding the playing field, evaluate it. Do you have what you need to get to where you'd like to be? What skills are you lacking or can sharpen? What is it that you need? Who or what has it, and how can you obtain it? Broaden your perspective and think about each playing field—relationships, partnerships, health, family, and work?

2. Knowing your **worth** and the value that you and your diversity bring. Girl, you are the table (an attraction), and on that menu (you have much to offer), and ready to serve (you're capable and prepared)! Understanding your worth is essential to preserving it and protecting your health.

3. Identify **toxicity** and protect your peace! Seriously, this is just a life hack. The sooner you can identify foolery, the sooner you can offset it. Revisit this lesson and fill in the blanks. Create a no-nonsense strategy for combating negativity and toxic people/places. "Breaking up" with toxic people and places is

freeing, and that relief will show. I promise you'll look much better in the face ☺.

4. **Managing stress** requires honesty, vulnerability, attention, and intentionality. Pay attention to your body, and how you feel. Verbalize what's going on with you (unapologetically) and prioritize your needs. The better you become at reducing stress in one area, the better you can become in another area.

5. **Setting boundaries** helps reduce stress and toxicity. Healthy boundaries are important for every area in your life. So, yup, please set them with everyone, including your children, parents, boo, bae, husband, family, and partner. Healthy boundaries also speak to healthy self-worth.

6. **Communities** are valuable simply because we were not created to be islands. One of my favorite Bible verses is Proverbs 11:14: "Where there is no counsel, the people fall; but in the multitude of counselors, there is safety."

Seriously, we won't perfect everything, and it may take time to even grasp or implement these principles. The goal is to make you aware and to inspire implementation to your personal and professional lives. In order to thrive, you must gain control of situations *before* they control you. Be more proactive and offensive vs. reactive and defensive. A wise person once told me the only thing that truly changes is change. Change is constant, and since we're aware of this, it's a great time to practice being open, honest, and knowledgeable of the need for change.

If your work environment is crappy and the chips are stacked against you and your ability to physically, mentally, or emotionally endure, it's time to make a change (whatever this is for you).

You can change your perspective, behaviors, or completely change your environment if it comes to that. Tip to survive and thrive: Keep your resume updated and ready to go. Each month, create a list of what you accomplished as an easy reference guide. This will make it easy to add items to your resume. Be sure to research best resume language and action verbs to better translate your task.

For instance, did you learn a new system, obtain new responsibilities, support someone, and/or learn a new role? Keeping a list will help you articulate your skills better. Time flies, and the worst thing that can happen is for an opportunity to arise, and you become stressed as you try to recall everything you have accomplished in order to update your resume.

Always have your resume updated and ready to send, even if you just finished a new employee orientation. Nothing is promised, and you can choose to leave or you can be let go your very first week of work. Be ready and stay ready, so you don't have to get ready. Seek new opportunities and remain vigilant.

Look for opportunities to grow, and keep in mind that learning is ongoing. The greater your personal and professional development, the more valuable you become to employers and the better equipped you are for new opportunities. Therefore, development and growth are things you should always strive for as a professional. When was the last time you invested in a course, workshop, seminar, or book (besides this one)? Most of us easily invest in makeup, hair, nails, entertainment, and wardrobes, but how often do we invest in our personal and professional development?

Yes, I need you to answer this question. Challenge your community with this, as well. And don't discredit the small lessons. Most principles and approaches correspond with other skills (transferable skills), so you may think, "Nah, I don't need this training," but you'll probably learn something from it—a strategy you can apply to both your profession and your everyday life. Therefore, stay motivated by learning new skills and identifying new talents you may have lying dormant inside of you. Try something new! You may be good at it.

Challenge

Locate three professional development opportunities, the dates, costs, and locations, and commit to attending at least one within the next 60 days. Write them down so it becomes a clearly defined goal.

Event Resources: Eventbrite, alumni groups, Facebook, Internet, LinkedIn or Instagram

Example: I will put aside $30 to attend "Be the Inspired You: Career and Professional Development workshop on

April 20, 2019. While there, I will intentionally network and exchange information with at least **three** people with the goal of possibly building a community with them.

_____

_____

_____

_____

_____

_____

_____

_____

We talked about personal mission statements and boundaries in Chapter Six. This is important for several reasons—not only for boundary-setting, but also for achieving individual deliverables. In addition to your personal mission statement, it's essential to have something similar for your career. Think about the bigger picture.

- Where do you want to be?
- Are you working for yourself or do you plan to retire from a company?
- Do you plan to work a couple of years (here and there) at multiple companies to gain a more diverse resume?
- Can you take the skills learned at your job and do this for yourself as an entrepreneur?
- Are you hoping to be in the C-suite or an SVP?

Identify three professional development goals. What are they?

_____

_____

_____

_____

_____

_____

_____

_____

_____

_____

_____

_____

Think about your career goals and write a personal career statement.

_____

_____

_____

_____

_____

_____

_____

_____

_____

_____

_____

Based on your career goals, plan accordingly. Everything in life will shift, as we talked about. You may only be at your current job for a season. Therefore, focus on your journey and what you can learn right now that will put you closer to your ultimate goal. In other words, do not become too wrapped up in the here-and-now. Instead, think about the bigger picture and what skills you can obtain right now that will align you with your personal mission statement and your career goals.

Learn to find value in each experience throughout your journey, and remember, Sis, that your journey will not look like anyone else's, so do *not* compare yours to someone else's. The grass isn't always greener, and everyone isn't who they post or portray themselves to be.

We talked about being on the menu and self-worth in Chapter Three. Self-worth helps to eliminate the comparison syndrome. I mean, we're all guilty of this in some form or fashion. It's normal to get sidetracked and compare your progress to that of others, but that will not help you thrive. And social media only amplifies the comparison trap—don't get sucked in! I recommend you spend some time with yourself and really learn who you are. Take inventory of your feelings in different situations. Do you tend to retreat or speak up in specific settings and situations? If you feel that you do one or both of these things, try to identify what triggered your change in behavior.

Be mindful and intentional about things that stimulate you and your passions. Speaking of passions, be sure to follow your heart as best you can. I believe that following our passions and our hearts are one and the same. I mean, you can't be passionate about something if it is not in your heart to do it. Therefore, pursuing your passion and following your heart produces a fulfillment like no other. Maybe you aren't in a position you're passionate about… maybe it's just a job to you. But it's *your* responsibility to learn something while you're there and to stimulate your passion. You would be doing yourself a great disservice by working nonstop in a mundane work environment without at least discovering something that stimulates your passion. Go out on the weekends, volunteer, or take up a trade or hobby. A healthy and holistic you is a you that pursues and stimulates her passions. Discover ways to merge your passions and interests with your career.

Mentorship is also essential for your transition from surviving to thriving. Aim to find a mentor, preferably someone 15-20 years older than you. They can be younger, but I feel that 15-20 years older is the best age. It's less likely an older mentor will feel threatened by you. In addition, having a mentor who is older than you are is mutually beneficial, given the different opinions, generations, and decades you grew up in. You will most likely provide a refreshed perspective and approach to things they *thought* they had mastered ☺. In turn, they can share perspective in areas you thought you knew. Do some scouting for your mentor, observe him/her, and then approach them. It never hurts to ask for support. Who knows? She/he might want to become part of your community.

Because they got to where they are with help, he/she may more than likely be willing to help you get where you want to be. Start small, with just a request for coffee or a few minutes of her time. Then, learn as much as you can about him/her. Learn how they got started and about the failures and lessons learned. It's so easy to get wrapped up in the victories that we neglect learning the important things that may help offset future mistakes. There are virtual mentors, as well. As a matter of fact, I listen to and watch several people from afar. However, my ideal mentor would be Oprah or someone like her. Okay, okay, so I'm dreaming…but I could use someone in her 60s who is professional, inviting, and God-fearing (shameless plug). Hey, you have to put it out there and be fearless in asking for what you need, right? *Right.*

How else will you thrive? Remember we are being honest, putting in the work, and manifesting our desires. Even YouTube speakers and random authors you'll probably never meet in real life can be a mentor. Check to see if this person is accessible anyway. See if you can reach him or her through email. Then shoot your shot and keep reaching out. You just never know; they may accept your offer. In the meantime, mentor others and stay connected to your community. Oh, and if at any time you feel you're outgrowing your community, or it's getting stale…Switch it up! You should always be growing and deliberate about surrounding yourself with individuals who are committed to doing the same. Sometimes people in your community are just there for an appointed time, and that's fine. For each new level, season, or space in your life, you will need a community that corresponds to where you are and where you're going. Now, your core friends and the permanent fixtures will not change as much, but others will, depending on your needs at any given time in your life.

In closing, nothing is permanent, and every work environment is temporary, especially if you are proactively looking to develop yourself. Keep your resume updated, eyes open, and if need be, simply move on. There is a department, organization, company, or business with your name on it. Seek opportunities, hire search agents, speak with recruiters and headhunters, and see what's out there.

Or create your own next opportunity. If you need motivation, act! Take action, even if you are not sure where to start. Action is motivation within itself. Action is manifestation. *Just start.* Things don't have to be perfect. Things don't have to be figured out in advance. Acting will also help encourage positive thoughts of future possibilities. In other words, acting gives the creator permission to step in. Furthermore, action is faith, and faith without work (or action) is dead. Lastly, don't let corporate beat you down. Don't let the hate of racism discourage, label, or box you in. Another person's ignorance is a reflection of them. You don't have to prove anything. Protect your peace and be exactly who you are…all of you! *I believe in you, Sis. You got this.*

BONUS

AFFIRMATIONS FOR THRIVING IN THE WORKPLACE

Hopefully, you've enjoyed, processed, and completed self-reflections after reading ***Woosah: A Survival Guide for Women of Color Working in Corporate***. More than anything, I hope you're empowered and equipped to make the transition from surviving to thriving.

I believe everything (e.g., a thought, image, idea, or whatever) starts in our minds; therefore, our brains are powerful beyond measure. I'm a witness that if you can change your mind, you can change your life. But, changing one's mind isn't as easy as it may sound. However, with a little work, intentionality, and practice, it is possible. Listen, I know all about it, but I truly believe that having a mindset shift is what ultimately changed my life—for the better.

In 2017, I lost four of my closest loved ones, all within eight months of each other. If that wasn't challenging enough, I took in two children after one of the deaths. The result? I became an "instant mom" practically overnight. And, because I was battling overwhelming grief, the stress of becoming a *single* mother so suddenly, work demands, life stressors, and anxiety—my health rapidly declined. I was in a difficult, dark space, battling clinical depression.

At times, the mere thought of getting out of bed and taking a shower was too much to bear. The vibrant person I once was no longer existed—at least for the time being. My "authentic self" was in hiding. But I knew I couldn't just lay there forever. Plus, to be honest, I just didn't have the guts to end it all. So, regardless of what was happening in my life, I *still* had to show up—at home and certainly at work, while wearing my corporate mask.

The things that helped shift my mindset the most were the affirmations and positive thoughts I repeated daily. These two things had a profound impact and influence on my thought processes. As a result, I began using my voice and advocating for myself. I had affirmations for *everything*, which is important because without them, I'm not sure I would even be here today. I repeated these affirmations and quotes religiously every day—in my home, with the kids, in emails, and even at work.

I also posted these affirmations in written form around my desk, on my computer monitors, my walls, and stashed in the center console of my car, so I could read them during my commute to and from work. I used them to purposely feed my mind with positivity. I saw, said, and affirmed myself in challenging areas—until I truly believed *everything* that came out of my mouth. The result? A shift in my mindset. Affirmations were my woosah method many times.

Affirmation is defined as emotional support or encouragement.

I believe affirmations are seeds for success. When planted properly, watered, and acted upon, mindsets evolve, producing a harvest of positive beliefs and changes in behavior—my gift to you.

Affirmations for Thriving in the Workplace

1. Where I am professionally is indicative of the work that I have or haven't put in...
2. My title does not define me. I am more than a title...
3. My value lies in my uniqueness...
4. I am capable, confident, competent, and assured of my skills...
5. The times I feel "not enough" are the times I will remind myself that I am more than enough...
6. Because I am more than enough, I am equipped to conquer every assignment, task, project, or obstacle that comes my way...
7. It is my responsibility to bring it *and* be the best version of myself...to the boardroom, conference room, office, and classroom...

8. No one is going to give me anything or do anything for me. If I want it, I have to take it, create it, build it, or work for it…

9. I will achieve greatness…

10. I did not make it this far just to quit, abort my mission, give in, fold, or fail…

11. My creator is with me every step of the way…

12. I am not for everyone, and that is fine. I will not take it personally…

13. I am sharp, intuitive, creative, and quick on my feet…

14. Absolutely no one else can bring what I bring…

15. I am bold, unapologetic, fearless, and unique…

16. I am a boss…

17. There are greater opportunities on the way to match my skills…

18. This is just a moment in time; nothing is permanent…

19. My thoughts are valuable *and* I will share them more often…

20. What can I learn from this?

21. My character, perspective, and behaviors are *not* contingent upon another person's values…

22. I will not take things personally or allow another person's problems to become mine…

23. I am a woman of integrity, regardless of what happens around me…

24. I was not created to "play it safe," "take it easy," or "dim my light" to make others feel comfortable…

25. I am *not* worried about reaping what I sow because I sow greatness…I am intentional about supporting others…

26. I am *not* intimidated, but rather, excited by challenges, because rising to the occasion stretches my skills and abilities and helps me grow…

27. If and when I fail (because I will), I will fail "forward," taking it in stride and walking away with a lesson that can be applied to my next challenge…

28. I will sometimes disappoint others, and that's okay because I know I can't please everyone. But I will still give it my all, every day…

29. My sistas are not my competition. *I* am my competition.

ABOUT THE AUTHOR

Rahkal Shelton Roberson is a multitalented author, dynamic speaker, certified professional life coach, workplace peace advocate, and CEO of Be The Inspired You, LLC, a personal and professional development business. With over fifteen years of combined experience in broadcast, project management, and education, Rahkal leverages her professional problem-solving, critical thinking, and strategic planning skills with her knack for creativity, solutions, and passion for serving others. Her uncanny ability to connect and educate is the foundation of her mission: serving, inspiring, and helping individuals confidently identify, own, and live out their God-given purpose.

Rahkal has a heart for professional development. As a coach, she helps women to obtain more fulfilling work experiences while cultivating smart and strategic career-planning moves. As a facilitator, she helps organizations become more sensitive and mindful of the needs of their human employees while creating harmonious work environments.

She is the author of *Woosah: A Survival Guide For Women of Color Working In Corporate*, *Woosah Workplace Peace A Workbook & Journal for Women of Color: 7 Keys To Obtaining A More Fulfilling Work Experience*, *Dreams Bigger Than Texas: A Story of Faith, Purpose, Perseverance, and Growth Into Womanhood*, and *Blackbird: The Story of a SistaMom*. Her work and expertise have been highlighted in *Forbes*, *HuffPost*, WGN, *Voyage Atl*, The Talk of Chicago, and Radio One.

Visit rahkalshelton.com to learn more.

REFERENCES

1. Lasswell, H. D. (2018). *Politics: Who gets what, when, how*. Pickle Partners Publishing.
2. Archer, C A. (2017). Injustice anywhere is injustice every-where: In honor of Dr. Martin Luther King Jr. *Huffpost*. Retrieved from https://www.huffpost.com/entry/injustice-anywhere-is-injustice-everywhere-in-honor_b_5879284fe4b03e071c14fcc0
3. U.S. Equal Employment Opportunity Commission. (2019). *Race/color discrimination*. Retrieved from https://www.eeoc.gov/laws/types/race_color.cfm
4. Jones, J. (2017). The racial wealth gap: How African-Americans have been shortchanged out of the materials to build wealth. *Economic Policy Institute*. Retrieved from https://www.epi.org/blog/the-racial-wealth-gap-how-african-americans-have-been-short-changed-out-of-the-materials-to-build-wealth/
5. American Institute of Stress. (2019). *Workplace stress*. Retrieved from https://www.stress.org/workplace-stress
6. Hunter-Gadsden, L. (2018). *The troubling news about black women in the workplace: What a LeanIn/McKinsey study found about mistreatment by managers*. Retrieved

from https://www.nextavenue.org/black-women-workplace/

7. Traub, A., Sullivan, L., Meschede, T., Shapiro, T. (2018). The Asset Value of Whiteness: Understanding the Racial Wealth Gap. *Demos*. Retrieved from https://www.demos.org/research/asset-value-whiteness-understanding-racial-wealth-gap

8. Cooke, P. (2007). Retrieved from https://www.phil-cooke.com/samuel_chand/

9. O'Brien, S. (2019). Here's how the wage gap affects black women. Retrieved from https://www.cnbc.com/2019/08/22/heres-how-the-gender-wage-gap-affects-this-minority-group.html

10. LeanIn.Org and McKinsey & Company. (2017 & 2018). Women in the Workplace. Retrieved from https://womenintheworkplace.com/

www.ingramcontent.com/pod-product-compliance
Lightning Source LLC
Chambersburg PA
CBHW031854200326
41597CB00012B/404